This book
belongs to

....

DINOSAURUS

The Ultimate Dinosaur Encyclopedia

This book was created by Quartz Editions for Zigzag Publishing
an imprint of Quadrillion Publishing Ltd.,
Woolsack Way, Godalming, Surrey GU7 1XW, U.K.

Consultant: Dr Paul Barret
General Editor: Tamara Green
Designer: Marilyn Franks
Illustrator: Tony Gibbons
Additional illustrations: Clare Heronneau
Cover Design by Sue Mims

This edition published in the U.S. in 1998 by
SMITHMARK Publishers, a division of U.S. Media Holdings,
Inc., 115 West 18th Street, New York,
NY 10011.

SMITHMARK books are available
for bulk purchase for sales promotion
and premium use. For details write or call the manager of special sales,
SMITHMARK Publishers,
115th West 18th Street,
New York, NY 10011.

Ref. No. 8566
10 9 8 7 6 5 4 3 2 1
Library of Congress Catalog Card Number: 98-60616
Printed and bound in India
ISBN 0-7651-0891-7

DINOSAURUS

The Ultimate Dinosaur Encyclopedia

SMITHMARK

Contents

Introduction

Welcome to this magnificently illustrated junior encyclopedia of dinosaurs, especially created to provide you with many hours of fascinating and informative entertainment.

As you read on, you'll find that this splendid work of reference is divided into four main sections. *Part 1*, entitled *When dinosaurs ruled*, begins in Triassic times, 220 million years ago when dinosaurs first evolved. Giant herbivores like Diplodocus and Brachiosaurus, you'll discover here, belong to the later Jurassic age; and not until the Cretaceous era did Tyrannosaurus rex start to rule supreme.

In *Part 2*, we present *Discovering dinosaurs*, all about the unearthing of some of the most famous finds. Be prepared for a few surprises here because dinosaurs have been discovered in all sorts of unexpected places and not only by paleontologists – experts in the study of fossils – but also by amateurs, even children as young as you are.

Remarkably, dinosaurs have been found on every continent, as *Part 3* – a *Dinosaur atlas* – goes to prove. And, finally, in *Part 4*, entitled *Dinosaur data*, we provide answers to some of the most frequent questions asked about the behavior of these prehistoric creatures.

What color were they? Which were the biggest? How long was their life span? And why did they finally become extinct?

Dinosaur names are fun to remember. But just in case you have any difficulty with them, at various points in this book, you'll find a guide as to how to pronounce them. And you can turn to our *Glossary* on page 254 if you come across any scientific words that you would like explained.

We trust you will enjoy dipping into the colorful pages that follow. Now begins a wondrous journey back in time, to long before human beings first existed ...

When dinosaurs

Life on Planet Earth began about 3,000 million years ago with tiny, single-celled creatures. And a huge span of time was to pass before dinosaurs eventually evolved about 220 million years ago, as shown at the top of this time line.

Not all dinosaurs lived at the same time: some types would die out, and other types would then evolve. But, in total, dinosaurs were around for as long as 160 million years.

In comparison, human beings like us have only been in existence for a very short while. In fact, dinosaurs ruled the world for over 50 times as long as humans have existed. That's why the boy at the end of the time ribbon takes up such a small space. Human beings and the dinosaurs were never contemporaries.

SUCCESSFUL SPECIES

How was it, then, that dinosaurs survived for so long, until their eventual extinction 65 million years ago? Scientists think one reason was that they adapted so well to their environment. Some dinosaurs were herbivores; others, carnivores – so there would have been enough food for them all. They were also well-suited to living on land and had tough skins.

Even baby dinosaurs had a good chance of survival because they hatched from hard-shelled eggs which protected them while they were developing prior to birth.

As you are about to discover when you turn the pages of this major section of the encyclopedia, some dinosaurs were huge, bulky-bodied and long-necked; others were hardly bigger than a turkey. Some were slow and plodding; others were as swift as gazelles.

NEW FINDS

Since the first dinosaur discoveries of the 19th century, many hundreds of different types have been unearthed. In fact, an entirely new find is currently made every seven weeks on average. Study the pages that follow and you will soon be as up-to-date as possible with current knowledge about the dinosaurs. Be sure to watch the newspapers, too, for details of any new finds that have perhaps been made this very week!

ruled

In Triassic times

As a volcano starts to erupt violently, producing showers of boiling hot lava, a herd of normally peaceful Mussaurus start to run for their lives. These are Late Triassic times, when dinosaurs first appeared and when such natural disasters were not at all unusual.

Planet Earth was very different about 220 million years ago, when dinosaurs first evolved. The world then consisted of one great ocean, known as Panthalassa (PAN-THAL-ASS-AH), and one huge landmass, Pangaea (PAN-JEE-AH).

Mussaurus lived in that part of Pangaea that we now call South America, before it broke away and became a separate continent. The climate was very hot then, and the landscape in many places was dry and somewhat desert-like. But after a rainstorm, an oasis of seed-ferns – plants that are now extinct, too – would sprout.

There was no grass as yet, nor any flowering plants. But horsetails, ginkgoes and conifers grew abundantly.

ANIMAL LIFE

Archosaurs (ARK-OH-SAWS) were abundant at this time. This group of advanced reptiles included crocodiles, flying reptiles and, of course, the dinosaurs, though only a few types existed as yet. Mussaurus was one of them, as you will discover in the section that follows. It lived peacefully for most of the time, alongside such creatures as early mammals and turtles. As an herbivore, however, it did not touch these for food. But the stillness was sometimes broken by the roar of a carnivore as it sought its next meal, or the cry of an early winged reptile flying overhead, warning that a predator was on the prowl.

Now read on and meet some of the other dinosaurs that lived during these times. As you will discover, their remains have been dug up in places that are as far apart as Argentina, the United States and Germany.

Coelophysis

A few scrappy remains of Coelophysis were first unearthed back in 1881. Then, in 1947, lots more fossils of Coelophysis were discovered in New Mexico – some of them the most perfect dinosaur skeletons ever found.

Coelophysis was small for a dinosaur – only around 10ft (3m) long, much of its body consisting of neck and tail. But even though not a giant, it was still a greedy carnivore and would attack for food, using its front limbs.

Strong jaws

CANNIBALS!

One of the first dinosaurs to appear on Planet Earth, Coelophysis is also one of the oldest dinosaurs that experts know well. But the most shocking discovery is that Coelophysis may have eaten its own kind. Indeed, scientists were amazed to find the bones of baby Coelophysis inside the ribcages of some of the adults.

Powerful back legs ————

LIVED: Late Triassic times
SIZE: 10ft (3m) long
WEIGHT: 44lb (20kg)
DISCOVERED: 1881, in USA

OTHER DATA: Carnivore; small; speedy; lightweight; may have hunted in packs; intelligent; cannibalistic; long, narrow jaws
NAME MEANS: "Hollow form"

Long, thin tail

Clawed fingers

World of Coelophysis

- Coelophysis was such a lightweight dinosaur that it would have been able to run easily at great speed on its long, slim back legs.

Coelophysis was definitely a dangerous predator; but in addition to other Triassic creatures, perhaps when food supplies ran short, seems to have used its small but razor-sharp teeth to eat its own young.

11

DINOSAUR DISASTER

One moment, hundreds of Coelophysis might have been happily hunting for food, as in the illustration *below*: the next, they could have been washed away in the most amazing flash flood. That, as far as paleontologists can tell, is the most likely scenario on a fateful Late Triassic day.

They have gathered this from the hundreds of Coelophysis skeletons found in New Mexico, USA. Normally, there would be safety in numbers, and others would join in to protect a Coelophysis if a larger carnivore attacked. But there would have been no escaping such an appalling natural disaster.

DINO FACT

Coelophysis would have been quick enough to catch passing winged insects, such as dragonflies, in its long, narrow jaws.

In such circumstances, the whole pack of Coelophysis would have drowned, together with any other small creatures that were at that spot – lizards and shrews, perhaps. Only the pterosaurs – winged reptiles soaring the Triassic skies – might have been able to fly to safety.

Mussaurus

LIVED: Late Triassic times
SIZE: 10ft (3m) long
WEIGHT: 330lb (150kg)
DISCOVERED: 1960, in Argentina

OTHER DATA: Quadrupedal; prosauropod; long neck; long tail; herbivore; tiny young
NAME MEANS: "Mouse lizard"

A Triassic and therefore very early dinosaur, Mussaurus was first identified from the skeletons of its young found in South America – some of the tiniest baby dinosaurs ever unearthed.

A typical prosauropod, Mussaurus had a small head, quite a long neck, a chunky body and a lengthy tail. Its hind limbs were thicker than the front ones, and it had five-toed feet.

As a prosauropod, Mussaurus would have had many small, leaf-shaped teeth lining its jaws for coping with the diet of an herbivore. Its teeth, however, were probably only used for breaking up vegetation into pieces that were small enough to be swallowed. It did not chew with its teeth. Rather, it swallowed small stones or *gastroliths* to help grind up the food in its stomach. Carnivores, however, did not need to aid digestion in this way.

RUNNING SCARED

Mussaurus could move around on all-fours or reach up into tall trees by standing on its hind limbs only. Most of the time, it just ambled along. But if danger approached, it was light enough to run for safety, though not at tremendous speed.

Given its name, meaning 'mouse lizard', because the first remains discovered were from mouse-size hatchlings, Mussaurus grew quickly and, within a few years, reached its full adult size.

MINI SKELETONS

The seven skeletons first discovered had skulls only 1in (3cm) long, and were huddled together in what looked like the remains of a nest where their bones had been very well preserved. Who would have thought that even baby dinosaur skeletons would have been small enough to be held in a human hand!

No one can be sure why the tiny baby Mussaurus died so young. It could be they had caught some prehistoric disease. Perhaps their mother had met with an accident and there was no one to care for them. Or maybe they were attacked by a predator. These are some of the possibilites experts have put forward.

World of Mussaurus

- Mussaurus grew to be about 20 times its birth size by the time it reached maturity. If you grew at that rate, you would end up about 25ft (7.6m) tall!

- It was one of an early dinosaur family, known as the Plateosaurids.

FATAL ENCOUNTER

You can see from the sequence of illustrations *below* just how dangerous a place the Triassic world was for herbivores like Mussaurus and their hatchlings.

The descripton that follows is of a typical encounter one Triassic day.

It was the middle of a very hot afternoon, and a mother Mussaurus was doing her best to shelter her newly-hatched babies from the rays of the scorching sun so that they did not get overheated. The baby dinosaurs were tiny, and had only just emerged from their shells. As yet, they had small appetites, but still needed to be fed.

DINO FACT

Mussaurus had lots of small leaf-shaped teeth which were ideal for coping with tough plant stuff.

This meant that their mother would have to plod down to a nearby oasis to find fresh vegetation to bring back for them. There, she would also be able to get a drink for herself.

The hatchlings watched her go and waited quietly. As yet they were too young even to romp about.

So the mother Mussaurus knew that they would be safe for a while.

Down at the pool, she drank her fill and splashed herself with water to freshen up. Feeling revived, she was now about to bite off some leaves for her offsprings' lunch, when the peace of the Triassic afternoon was suddenly interrupted by the roar of the earliest known dinosaur, Staurikosaurus (STORE-EEK-OH-SAW-RUS) — a carnivore far more ferocious than the plant-eating mother Mussaurus but smaller than her species.

Taking the Mussaurus completely by surprise, the meat-eater sprang at her, knocking the new mother on her side. She would not survive this attack. And without her to tend them, her hatchlings would not live long either.

DINO FACT

Most remains of the very first dinosaurs, from Late Triassic times, have been found in South America.

17

Procompsognathus

One of the smallest dinosaurs discovered so far, Procompsognathus is also one of the 'stars' of *The Lost World*, Michael Crichton's sequel to *Jurassic Park*, in which dinosaurs are "brought back to life."

In spring 1909, paleontologists digging in a stone quarry near a town called Heilbron in Germany came across some fascinating remains.

They had not unearthed a complete skeleton, but the broken parts of a skull, right leg, hip and other fossilized bones found were enough to show that this was an entirely new dinosaur. What was more, it was one dating from Triassic times, when dinosaurs first evolved. Later given the name Procompsognathus, it is one of several different-looking species of dinosaurs that have been discovered in this part of Europe.

SMALL AND RARE

The skeletons of small, lightweight dinosaurs broke up fairly easily and quickly after they died, but the bones of big dinosaurs were much tougher.

This is probably why so few fossil fragments of small dinosaurs have been found, in comparison with the number of skeletons of larger dinosaurs that have been unearthed.

Small dinosaurs may have had a shorter life span than their giant cousins, too. Many would also have fallen prey to larger species, proving easy targets because of their small size.

TINY BABIES

Procompsognathus was exceedingly small by dinosaur standards. Just imagine how tiny its newly born hatchlings would have been – hardly bigger than a mouse, perhaps.

World of Procompsognathus

- Halticosaurus (HAL-TICK-OH-SAW-RUS) was a larger early carnivore and a contemporary of Procompsognathus.

- Another contemporary was Plateosaurus (PLAT-EE-OH-SAW-RUS), a long-necked herbivore many times Procompsognathus' size.

LIVED: Late Triassic times
SIZE: 4ft (1.2m) long
WEIGHT: 2lb (1kg)
DISCOVERED: 1909, in Germany

OTHER DATA: Bipedal mostly; primitive carnivore; predatory; very small for a dinosaur; long slim head; lengthy tail
NAME MEANS: "Before Compsognathus"

19

GETTING IT TOGETHER

When paleontologists find scattered remains instead of a complete skeleton, their task is like trying to solve a jigsaw puzzle. The problem is made worse because they have no illustration on a box to guide them as they try to put the bones together.

Long jaws —

Many pieces may also be missing. They therefore have to use both their knowledge and imagination to get an idea of what the dinosaur may have looked like all those millions of years ago.

Scientists have found very few remains of this miniature species. An artist's reconstruction

DINO FACT

Scientists think that Procompsognathus possibly often feasted on the remains of animals killed by larger dinosaurs.

of Procompsognathus' skeleton has therefore been based upon both the fossilized bones that have been discovered and also the remains of similar dinosaurs. What, then, has been learned from these fragments of Procompsognathus?

SHARP-TOOTHED

Procompsognathus was certainly small and may even have made a good pet if it had survived to the present day. The main disadvantage to having it around, however, would have been that it could probably have given a nasty bite.

Its jaws were probably very long for a creature of such a small size, and they would have been lined with lots of tiny teeth – maybe twice as many as *you* have in *your* mouth. These would have been very sharp. In fact, they were ideal for a creature with a daily diet of raw flesh.

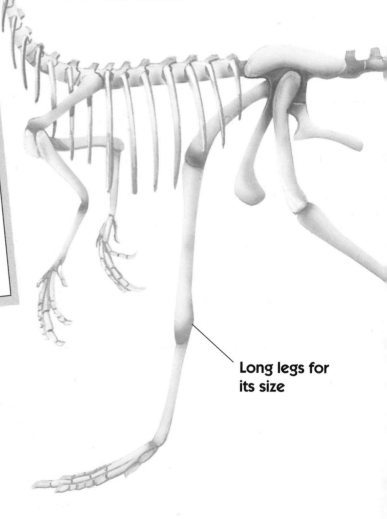

Long legs for its size

LITTLE AND LIGHT

Scientists know that Procompsognathus' skeleton must have been lightweight because its bones were slim instead of sturdy. Indeed, it probably weighed only about as much as a football. We also know that Procompsognathus must have been bipedal. This means that it walked around on two legs instead of four. We can tell this because of the great difference between the size of its front and hind limbs.

DINO FACT

We do not know for sure what sort of sound Procompsognathus produced, but it was more than likely fairly high-pitched.

But the dinosaurs Procompsognathus and Compsognathus (<u>KOMP</u>-SOG-<u>NAY</u>-THOOS) differed in a number of ways.

The Triassic dinosaur Procompsognathus was given its name, meaning "before Compsognathus," by a famous paleontologist named Eberhard Fraas. Compsognathus was also found in Germany but in far later Jurassic rock strata.

Thin tail

Experts believe Procompsognathus probably had five fingers on each hand, and that two of these were shorter than the others and used as thumbs. These may have helped Procompsognathus grasp the insects and other small creatures that it caught for food.

PRETTY JAW

They may have very similar names; they were certainly both small carnivores; and they were very much alike in their overall body structure.

The new discovery's name meant "pretty jaw," and so Procompsognathus' name therefore *really* means "before pretty jaw." Both were definitely better-looking than some prehistoric monsters; but it is unlikely that they seemed very "pretty" to those creatures falling victim to the sharp teeth of these mini predators.

Only two Compsognathus skeletons have been unearthed so far. These show that it was about 2ft 6in (75cm) long – smaller than Procompsognathus. It has even been described as chicken-like in size. Indeed, so bird-like was Compsognathus that scientists once confused its remains with the first bird, Archaeopteryx (ARK-EE-OPT-ER-ICKS).

In Jurassic times

It was during Jurassic times, which lasted from 208-145 million years ago approximately, that giant plant-eaters such as Brachiosaurus, on the right of this illustration, roamed the plains of Planet Earth.

Sauropods, like Brachiosaurus, were some of the tallest forms of life the world has ever known. Browsing on the highest trees, they would trample great paths through ferns growing thickly on the ground, leaving trails of footprints.

They also left piles of droppings, the result of all the plant stuff that they ate. The weather in Jurassic times was warmer and wetter than it is today. Vegetation was therefore lush and ideal for greedy plant-eaters. In fact, many types of dinosaurs had evolved by this time.

Dryosaurus

Stegosaurus

Dryosaurus (DRY-OH-<u>SAW</u>-RUS), for instance – the smallest, shown *below left*, was a fast runner and could make an easy escape if a predator, such as Allosaurus, shown *opposite*, threatened it. The Kentrosaurus (KENT-ROH-<u>SAW</u>-RUS), to the *bottom right*, was a smaller cousin of Stegosaurus, shown *center*. Both were herbivores and had plated backs and spikes as weaponry. Yet they, too, constantly had to be on their guard. Carnivorous dinosaurs could be hiding in the thickets.

Here, they would wait to ambush their victims. In the section that follows, we introduce many of the dinosaurs that roamed the Jurassic world. Read on and get wise to what they looked like and how they lived.

Brachiosaurus

Kentrosaurus

23

Allosaurus

A true giant, from the tip of its tail to the end of its snout, Allosaurus was as long as three of today's average-sized cars and an exceedingly ferocious carnivore.

Seen here, about to attack a victim, Allosaurus had all the features of a typical carnosaur – a big head, small front limbs, strong back legs, clawed feet and a lengthy tail. But, of course, the most dangerous things about Allosaurus were its giant jaws and fangs.

The first part of Allosaurus to be dug up was a piece of tail bone, discovered in 1869. Not until several years later were other remains belonging to the same animal found. It was then named Allosaurus, meaning "strange reptile."

Clawed feet

Powerful legs

LIVED: Late Jurassic times
SIZE: 36ft (11m) long
WEIGHT: 1.5 tons
DISCOVERED: 1869, in USA

OTHER DATA: Bipedal; carnivore; thick neck; small but strong arms; clawed hands and feet; huge teeth; powerful legs; mighty tail
NAME MEANS: "Strange reptile"

A complete skeleton was discovered at The Cleveland-Lloyd Dinosaur Quarry in the state of Utah, USA, in 1883, but the richest excavations took place more recently between 1960 and 1965.

POWERFUL LEGS

Allosaurus' legs had to be very strong to support all its body weight. On its feet, the first toe faced backward; the other three, forward. Some experts think this was possibly advantageous, helping Allosaurus to carry its colossal weight more readily.

Large jaws

World of Allosaurus

- Most Allosaurus finds have been made in the state of Utah, USA.

- Allosaurus was the most common predator of Jurassic times.

Compared with its legs, however, Allosaurus' arms were small. Still, they are likely to have been strong, ending in three terrible curved claws, useful for gripping prey.

Allosaurus' body was bulky and ended in a long, thick but tapering tail that helped it to balance. As you can see, it was held off the ground as Allosaurus moved or fought.

Many dinosaur bones have special marks on them, called "muscle attachment scars." By studying these, scientists can tell how the muscles were attached to each bone. If they then compare their findings with what is known about today's animals, they can get a very good impression of how the dinosaur behaved. This is, in fact, how we know that Allosaurus was so powerful.

JAWS!

The most terrifying thing about Allosaurus was its huge mouth. It was lined with sharp teeth which curved backward, making them perfect for tearing flesh from unfortunate victims. It also meant that Allosaurus could hang on tightly to its prey if the creature struggled to escape an imminent death.

GREEDY MONSTER

How, then, did Allosaurus actually feed? First, it would grab a chunk of flesh in its mouth. Then the upper jaw pulled backward to slice at the meat with Allosaurus' large, razor-sharp teeth. Next, the jaws would move outward, widening the mouth so that Allosaurus could swallow as much as possible in one giant gulp. It was a fearfully greedy predator.

Allosaurus never chewed its food but downed its meat in great chunks. It would even swallow small animals whole and could undoubtedly have eaten *you* in just one bite – if humans had existed back in Jurassic times. So that Allosaurus could cope with such large lumps of flesh, without risk of choking, its gullet could probably stretch like elastic.

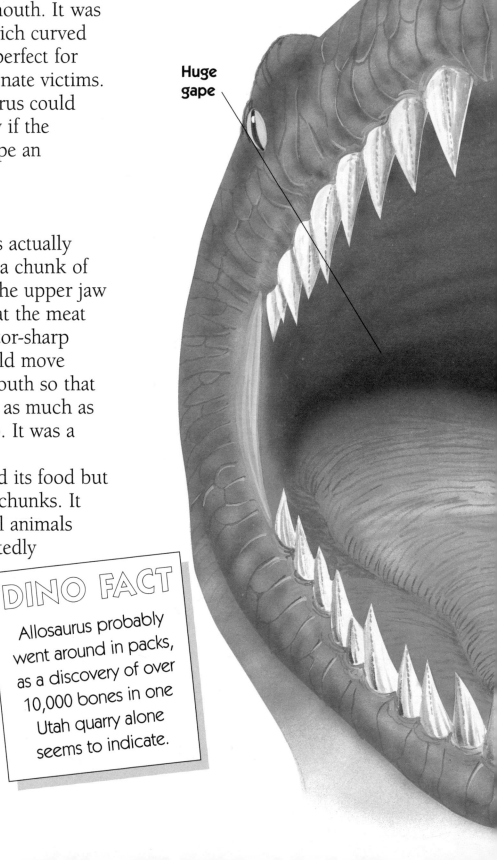

Huge gape

DINO FACT

Allosaurus probably went around in packs, as a discovery of over 10,000 bones in one Utah quarry alone seems to indicate.

26

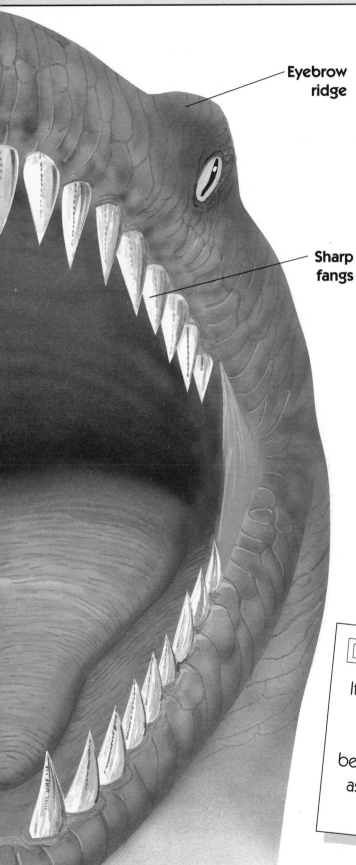

Eyebrow ridge

Sharp fangs

LIGHT-HEADED

Allosaurus' head may seem to have been very big but it was actually quite light because of spaces between the bones. There were also powerful muscles in Allosaurus' neck and back that helped to operate its horrifying jaws. Allosaurus could therefore move its head around very easily – all the better to grab at its prey. As for the sight of such a huge, gaping mouth, that must have been truly terrifying!

EYEBROW RIDGES

Above each eye, Allosaurus had a prominent ridge made of bone. What is rather strange is that the center of it seems to have been hollow. No one is quite sure why this would have been so. Some paleontologists, however, have suggested that it may have contained a salt gland originally, The function of this gland could have been to help balance Allosaurus' salt level. Another possible theory is that the ridges were larger in males to attract the females. In fact, one of the principal ways to distinguish an Allosaurus skull from that of a T rex is through the presence of these eyebrow ridges.

DINO FACT

Its throat bones show that Allosaurus' tongue must have been enormously long, as well as extremely wide and thick.

Apatosaurus

To a huge Apatosaurus, weighing more than 20 tons – as much as four adult elephants – you would have seemed as small as a kitten. Mostly, however, it lived a calm and peaceful life.

In Late Jurassic times, when herds of the enormous but gentle herbivore Apatosaurus (formerly known as Brontosaurus) roamed vast plains between the forests and mountains of what is now North America, alongside other sauropods, the weather was much warmer and wetter than now.

LIVED: Late Jurassic times
SIZE: 70ft (21m) long
WEIGHT: 20 tons
DISCOVERED: 1877, in USA

OTHER DATA: Quadrupedal; herbivore; small head; long, tapering tail; heavy legs; once called "Brontosaurus"
NAME MEANS: "Deceptive lizard"

Cycads, ferns and ginkgoes, as well as horsetails and enormous conifers, grew near swampy riverbanks. Such lush vegetation was ideal for greedy herbivores. Apatosaurus' main choice was between the low-lying plants that surrounded rivers and lakes and the leaves of tall trees.

It had a very healthy appetite, eating tons of foliage each week; but luckily, it could cross stretches of water in search of more foodstuff on the other side, without risk of drowning because of its tremendous height.

29

LONG-NECKED SKELETON

As you can see from the reconstruction shown here, Apatosaurus' head was very small compared with its body size, and its brain was tiny, too.

Very long neck

This indicates that it was more than likely not very intelligent but, then, it probably did not need to be. As an herbivore, Apatosaurus was quite happy spending its days browsing in the treetops and looking for juicy leaves, rather than stalking prey for its supper as a carnivore would have had to do.

Apatosaurus' skull had eye sockets set far back, and long, slim teeth at the front of its snout for raking up plant stuff. Paleontologists have also noticed that its nostrils were placed quite high on its head – possibly to stop branches going up its nose when feeding.

From Apatosaurus' small head stretched a great long neck. Since you would only have reached its shins, *you* would have had to stretch *your* neck as far as possible just to get a glimpse of Apatosaurus' head!

DINO FACT

An Apatosaurus footprint would have been both wide and long enough for two children to sit in comfortably.

World of Apatosaurus

- The large claw on Apatosaurus' inner toes was probably used as a defense weapon at times, when it needed to deter a predator.

- Just as your sneakers have padded soles, some scientists think that Apatosaurus' feet had special padding to provide support and prevent damage.

Apatosaurus' leg bones had to be extremely strong to support all that body weight. Oddly, paleontologists have found some Apatosaurus tracks that seem to be of their front limbs only. It is thought these tracks may be in places where rivers and lakes once existed.

Apatosaurus may have tried to cross the water, using their front limbs to haul themselves along, while the rest of the body floated. Their tails could have been used to propel them through the water, too. And such a long, tapering tail was no doubt functional if an enemy approached. Apatosaurus could wield it like a whip to strike a nasty blow.

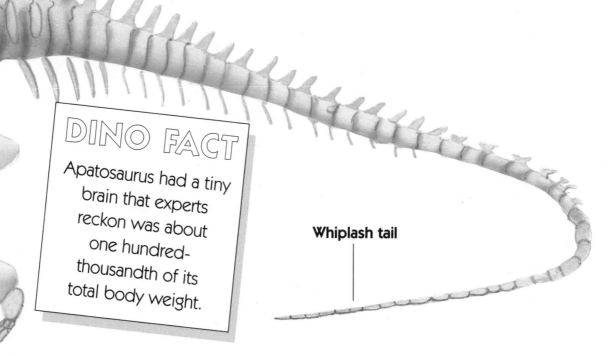

DINO FACT

Apatosaurus had a tiny brain that experts reckon was about one hundred-thousandth of its total body weight.

Whiplash tail

Brachiosaurus

Brachiosaurus was a giant, one of the biggest and heaviest dinosaurs that ever lived. Yet it was gentle by nature and would not attack unless provoked by a predator.

Long, crane-like neck

Human beings did not exist, of course, when Brachiosaurus roamed Planet Earth all those millions of years ago.

Broad round feet at the end of straight, thick legs

LIVED: Late Jurassic times		**OTHER DATA:** Herbivore; long-necked; longer front limbs; huge appetite; lived in herds; raised head crest; large strides	
SIZE: Up to 77ft (23m) long			
WEIGHT: 50 tons		**NAME MEANS:** "Arm lizard"	
DISCOVERED: 1900, in USA			

But if they had, a fully-grown man would have found that he hardly reached this colossal creature's knees. Brachiosaurus, meanwhile, could very easily stretch its enormously long neck right up to the top of the tallest trees.

Brachiosaurus was as long as a tennis court and weighed as much as several elephants.

Just like today's elephants, too, under each foot it had a thick, cushioned pad to protect its bones from jarring as it plodded about at a slow pace and with tremendous strides.

MASSIVE MEALS

Brachiosaurus only ate plants and must have gobbled down a huge amount of food to provide enough energy for its enormous body. As a result, its droppings probably formed the most colossal heaps!

Strong, bulky body

High nostrils

Small head

World of Brachiosaurus

- Brachiosaurus spent most of its time feeding on conifers, cycads and ferns.

- Its young probably took 10 years or more to grow to full adult size and may have lived to over 70.

- Brachiosaurus' powerful tail was possibly used as a weapon at times.

- Brachiosaurus had a tiny brain and so scientists think it was probably not very intelligent.

Brachiosaurus probably lived in families or groups of up to 20 dinosaurs, as paleontologists have discovered from their many fossilized tracks.

FACING DANGER

Monsters, such as Allosaurus, were continually on the prowl, ever hungry for a meal of Brachiosaurus meat. But in the face of such danger, a sturdy Brachiosaurus might have tried to deal a nasty blow to the hopeful predator with one whack of its long tail.

With luck, the assailant would be brought to the ground before it had a chance to steal one of the young.

A newly-hatched Brachiosaurus was tiny in comparision with its parents and probably had a soft skin that only hardened and became more scaly as it grew to maturity.

Powerful tail, balancing the weight of its neck

DINO FACT

The most complete Brachiosaurus skeleton found so far is from Tanzania, Africa, and is now on display in a German museum.

34

As Brachiosaurus walked, it must have held its legs very straight. Being so heavy, if it had bent its legs a lot, the bones might have fractured easily under all that weight.

Large nostrils

Long body

Small, soft-skinned hatchlings

35

Ceratosaurus

It is hardly surprising that Ceratosaurus is sometimes thought to have looked much like the dragons in storybooks. Just look at its odd nose horn and peculiar eye ridges!

Remains of Ceratosaurus were first discovered in 1883 by a paleontologist named M.P. Felch in a quarry in Fremont County, Colorado, in the United States. Since then, not many remains have been found. However, scientists have still been able to piece together a sufficient number of its fossilized bones to produce a fairly good picture of what Ceratosaurus must have looked like.

HUNTER'S SKELETON

The skeleton of Ceratosaurus, experts agree, is essentially that of a well-designed hunter and meat-eater. Its skull was quite large, and most of it consisted of jaws that were almost as big as those of an Allosaurus.

We do not know exactly how Ceratosaurus hunted, however. It may have done so on its own, hiding behind trees, perhaps, and then jumping out to surprise passing prey. Some scientists, though, think Ceratosaurus may have hunted in small packs.

When Ceratosaurus attacked its victims – such as the young Camarasaurus (KAM-AR-A-SAW-RUS) shown *here* – it may first have dug its teeth into the animal. Then, using its powerful neck muscles, it may have ripped off pieces of flesh from its prey.

Ceratosaurus also probably used its strong arms to hold its prey down as the victim struggled. But, like many other carnivores, Ceratosaurus may also have eaten the remains of any dead animals it found.

Eyebrow ridges

Nose horn

Camarasaurus

Four-fingered hands

LIVED: Late Jurassic times
SIZE: 20ft (6m) long
WEIGHT: 1 ton
DISCOVERED: 1883, in USA

OTHER DATA: Carnivore; bipedal; huge head; eye ridges; nose horn; clawed hands and feet; broad tail
NAME MEANS: "Horned lizard"

World of Ceratosaurus

- Tanzania, in central Africa, as well as western North America, were home to Ceratosaurus-like dinosaurs in Late Jurassic and possibly also Early Cretaceous times.

So ever-hungry Ceratosaurus may have been a scavenger at times, as well as a savage killer.

Either way, we know that Ceratosaurus did not have much trouble swallowing huge chunks of meat. Its skeleton shows that the skull was built to expand sideways, so that its enormous and terrifying jaws could open very wide.

Strong tail

Clawed feet

SIZE PUZZLE

We have a fairly accurate idea of Ceratosaurus' appearance. But some things about it remain a mystery. What, for instance, was its overall size? Some skeletons show that the dinosaur was about 20ft (6m) long. Other bones that have been found, however, point to it having been quite a bit larger, while others suggest it was smaller. Perhaps, however, these skeletons were at different stages of growth.

DINO FACT

Ceratosaurus had clawed four-fingered hands at the end of its short arms but only three-toed feet, also clawed.

Bony ridges

Nose horn

Huge, sharp teeth

DINO FACT

Ceratosaurus' tail was mostly stiff but quite supple at the end so that it could be shaken from side to side when in combat.

HORNY PROBLEM

Experts are still not certain about certain aspects of the horn on Ceratosaurus' snout either. It could have been used to butt rival males; or it may simply have been very large on a male Ceratosaurus so that it could impress the females prior to mating. Then again, perhaps the size of its horn was an indication of the dinosaur's age, the horn getting bigger as it got older. It has even been debated that Ceratosaurus may have nodded its head up and down very vigorously at times in order to show off its nose horn.

RIDGE RIDDLES

The bony ridges over its eyes provide yet another riddle. They could have afforded useful protection to the eyes when Ceratosaurus fought; or maybe, again, they were simply attractive to the opposite sex.

As for the narrow row of bony plates along Ceratosaurus' back that stood up like a low ridge, no one knows the purpose of this either. It certainly does not seem to have been large enough to protect a Ceratosaurus from its enemies; so maybe it was purely ornamental. If only paleontologists could find further remains of Ceratosaurus, maybe all or some of these puzzles could be solved. But it could be we shall never know for sure.

Dilophosaurus

Known for its strange, bony, double-crested head, Dilophosaurus was a lightly-built but fierce and rather ugly-looking carnivore that roamed parts of what is now North America.

There was great excitement back in 1942 when a number of fascinating dinosaur remains were discovered in northern Arizona, in the United States. They were found by a team of paleontologists from the University of California, who had been shown the site by a Navajo named Jesse Williams.

THREE MYSTERY SKELETONS

As the team started to dig at the site, they slowly uncovered three skeletons. One was almost complete, measuring about 20ft (6m) long, but it had no skull, so no one could tell what its head would have been like. The other two skeletons were in lots of pieces, and much of the bones had been worn away over millions of years. The experts wondered which species of dinosaurs they could possibly have belonged to.

MAJOR MISTAKE

The American paleontologist, Samuel P. Welles, worked very hard at putting the bones together, but then made a big error. He thought that they must have belonged to a Megalosaurus. This was probably because the skull was missing. Apart from that, some of the bones of a Dilophosaurus and a Megalosaurus are admittedly quite similar.

Then, many years later, Welles found another such skeleton, only this time it was in better condition and had its skull intact, complete with a pair of the bony crests that, today, are taken to identify a Dilophosaurus. Welles now realized that it was a totally different creature after all. Later, in 1970, Welles gave his dinosaur the name that we now know it by – Dilophosaurus, meaning "two-ridged lizard," because of the double crest that crowned its head.

World of Dilophosaurus

- It seems that Dilophosaurus may have lived in groups or packs, and that the largest-crested male would lead the small herd.

- There is a magnificent Dilophosaurus skeleton at the University of California Museum of Paleontology, Berkeley, USA.

LIVED: Early Jurassic times
SIZE: 20ft (6m) long
WEIGHT: 880lb (400kg)
DISCOVERED: 1942, in USA

OTHER DATA: Bipedal; carnivore; clawed hands and feet; double, bony crest; stiff, tapering tail; sharp teeth
NAME MEANS: "Two-ridged lizard"

SPITTING IMAGE

In the movie *Jurassic Park*, there is a scary scene in which a Dilophosaurus stars. The dinosaur suddenly aims a jet of dreadful-looking venom at a computer expert working in the theme park who had stolen some embryos being made in a laboratory. But was Dilophosaurus *really* able to spit poison? No one knows, but some snakes living today can certainly defend themselves in this way.

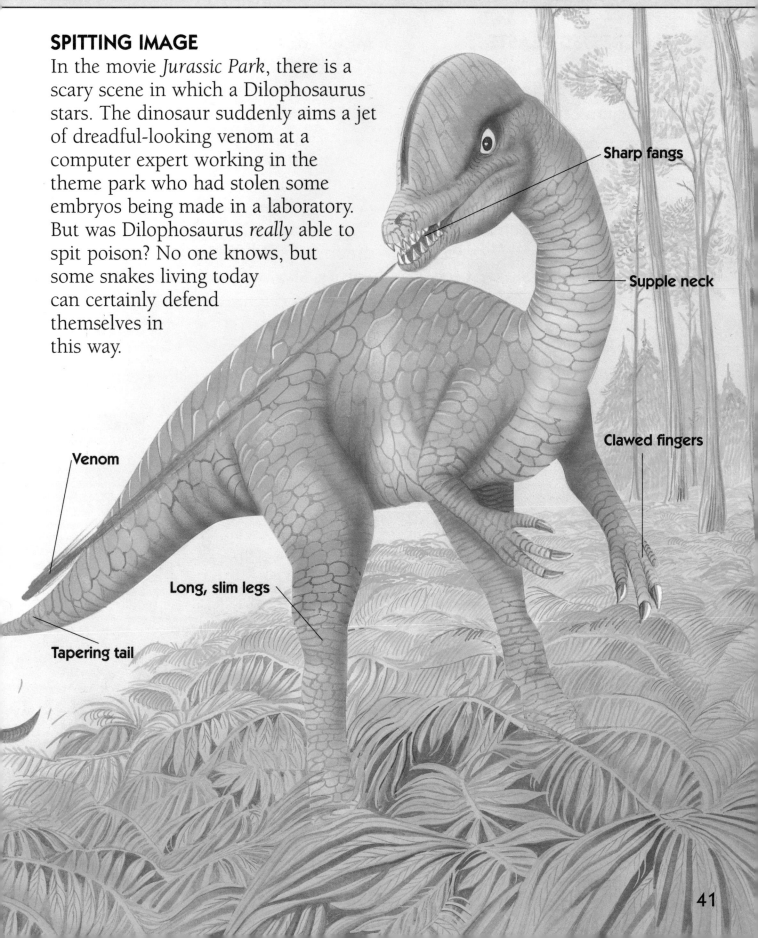

Sharp fangs

Supple neck

Clawed fingers

Venom

Long, slim legs

Tapering tail

41

DOUBLE-CRESTED BEASTS

Dilophosaurus' crests looked much like two halves of a dinner plate lying side by side, and running from the front to the back of the skull. No one knows their function for certain. They may have been brightly colored in the males for sexual display, or perhaps had some sort of part to play in controlling temperature. They were certainly too delicate to have been useful as effective weapons.

MEAN MEAT-EATER

Dilophosaurus was a fierce carnivore, grabbing a large meal of meat wherever it could find one. Some scientists even believe that it may have scavenged just as frequently as it killed for its food, as in the illustration *below*. So it may sometimes have fed on dead animals that it found lying around – such as the Diplodocus' corpse, shown here – rather than lying in wait to catch its supper.

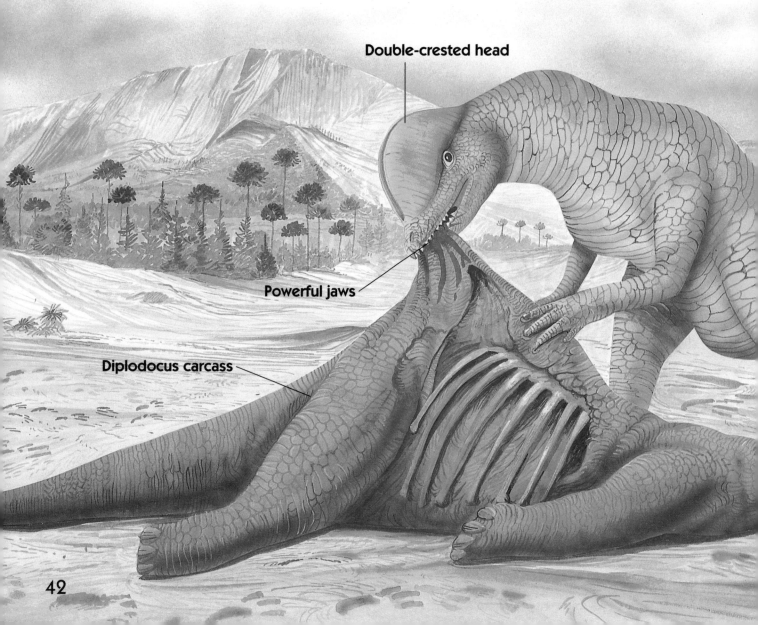

Double-crested head

Powerful jaws

Diplodocus carcass

FROM CLAWS TO JAWS

Dilophosaurus' jaws may simply not have been sufficiently powerful to deal with huge, violently struggling creatures that came its way. Its hands were quite large, however. Three of the four fingers on each had sharp claws and these would have been ideal for tearing meat.

Then its jaws could take over and get down to the serious business of gulping down a meal.

Of course, if Dilophosaurus was very hungry and saw a small, tasty-looking creature – such as the armored, plant-eating creature in the scene *below* – it would probably have gone after it right away because such a pint-sized victim would surely have fallen prey to its clutches.

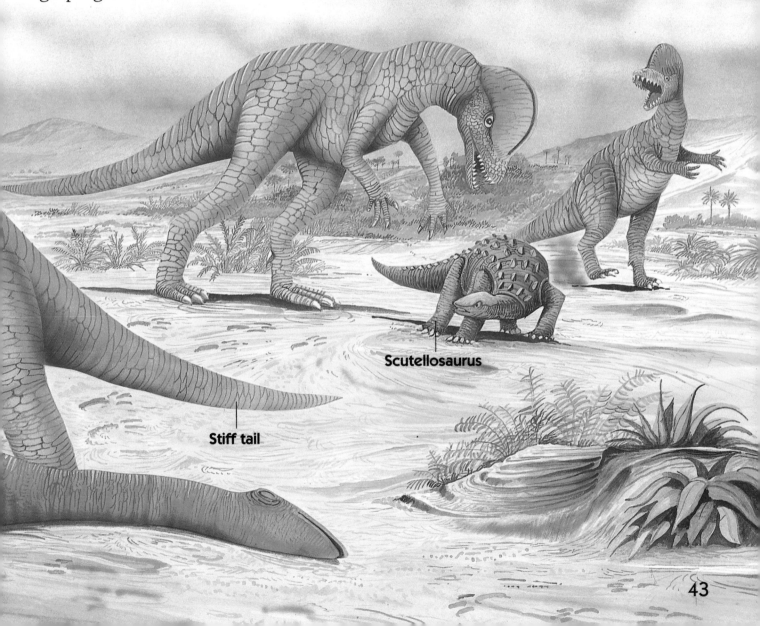

Scutellosaurus

Stiff tail

Diplodocus

Tiny dinosaurs were dwarfed by a huge plant-eater like Diplodocus, and probably frequently risked being trampled on.

Torso

Longer even than a tennis court, Diplodocus was a massive and very muscular herbivore that was, by and large, very peaceful, although not very nimble or intelligent. So it had to be constantly on the look-out.

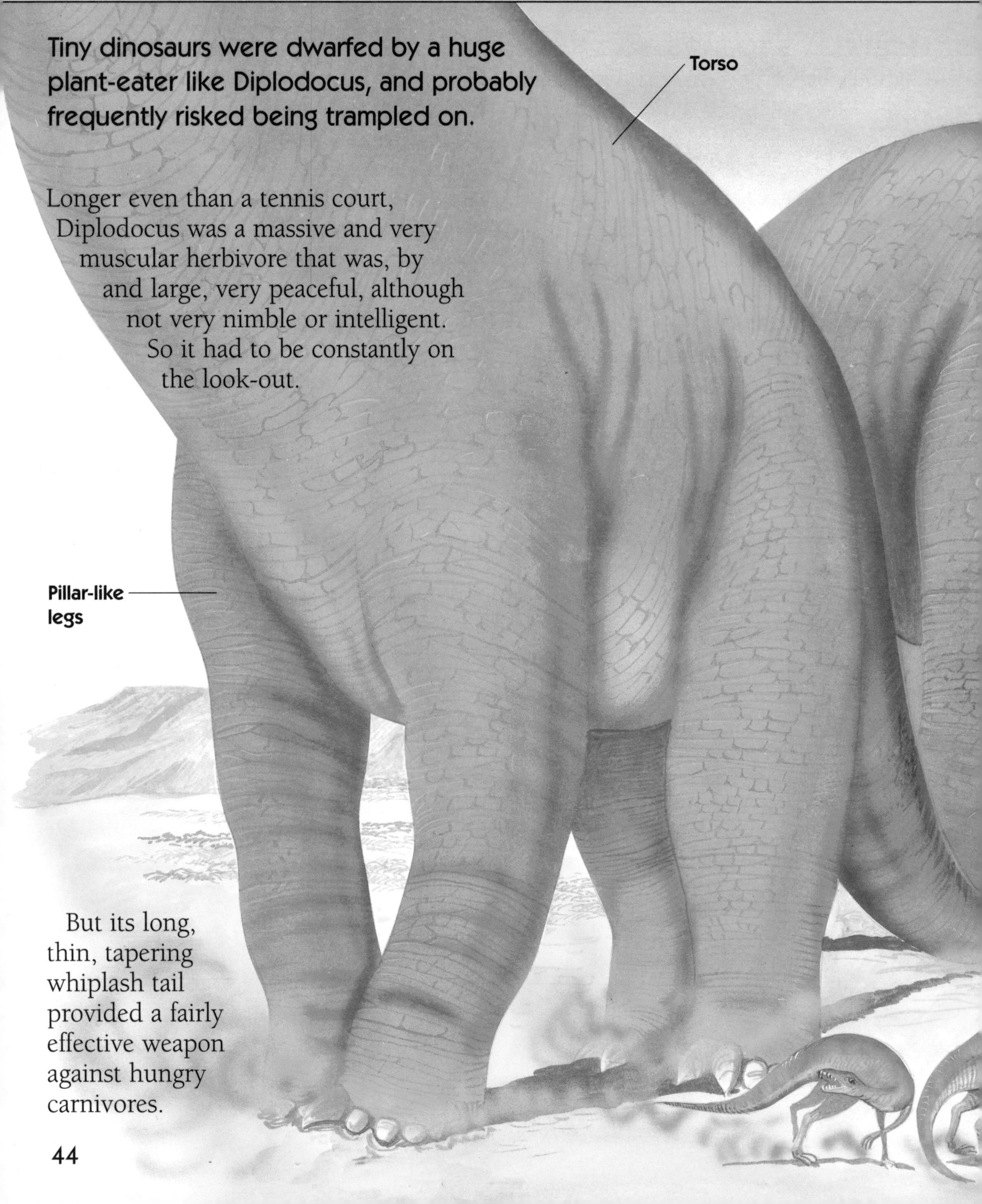

Pillar-like legs

But its long, thin, tapering whiplash tail provided a fairly effective weapon against hungry carnivores.

44

LIVED: Late Jurassic times
SIZE: 87ft (27m) long
WEIGHT: 10 tons
DISCOVERED: 1877, in USA

OTHER DATA: Herbivore; small head; very long whiplash tail; huge limbs; snake-like neck; lightweight skeleton
NAME MEANS: "Double beam"

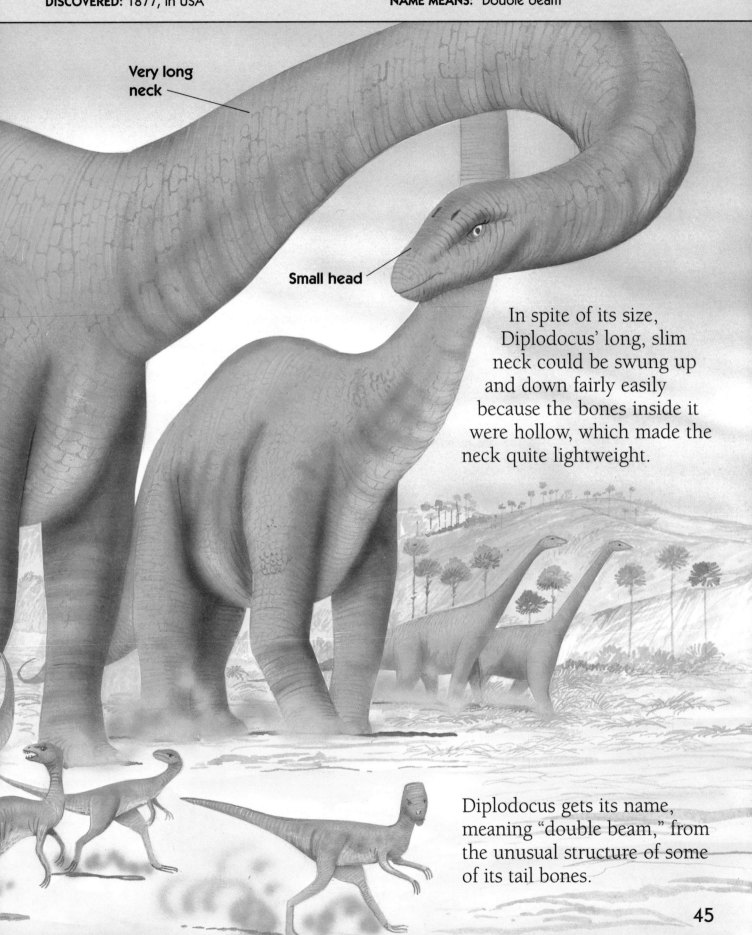

Very long neck

Small head

In spite of its size, Diplodocus' long, slim neck could be swung up and down fairly easily because the bones inside it were hollow, which made the neck quite lightweight.

Diplodocus gets its name, meaning "double beam," from the unusual structure of some of its tail bones.

45

SALAD DAYS

Herds of Diplodocus traveled across the Jurassic landscape, constantly looking for leaves and plants on which to feed, and eating from the tallest trees which other smaller dinosaurs could not reach. Once they had stripped one part of a forest, they would then move on to find new feeding grounds. For such huge dinosaurs, any time was feeding time.

Diplodocus had pencil-like teeth at the front of its mouth – not ideally suited to chewing. However, it probably swallowed pebbles or tiny stones, too.

DIP-LOD-OH-KUS

Its eyes were about 9ft (3m) above the ground and set on either side of its head. It would therefore have had a wonderful panoramic view of the landscape around it, as depicted in this illustration of a few Diplodocus feeding while a predator approaches. With such a very long neck, it may have been able to spot such enemies from afar and make a quick get-away.

It used these pebbles to grind up its food internally into small pieces that could then be digested.

Have you ever wondered what the world must have looked like to a Diplodocus?

Megalosaurus

Join us as we go on a dinosaur trek and find out just how horrific an encounter with a huge meat-eater like Megalosaurus must have been.

Time and again, Megalosaurus let out a terrifying roar. It was a steaming hot Jurassic afternoon, and the hungry dinosaur's temper was flaring. It had not eaten since early morning, and the prospect of a meal of Cetiosaurus (SEE-TEA-OH-SAW-RUS) was irresistable. However, the large herbivore seemed determined to fight back.

Equally angry, it struck out at the carnivore with its long tail. In spite of its great height, it was terrified of the smaller meat-eater and somehow sensed it might end up as its dinner.

Cetiosaurus was one of the earliest dinosaurs to be discovered. First unearthed in England in the 19th century, it was an early sauropod. But it had an unusually solid, heavy backbone. No wonder it was able to deal Megalosaurus such a mighty blow.

BLOODY BATTLE
In retaliation, Megalosaurus snarled furiously and leapt up to take a huge bite out of Cetiosaurus' side. It was indeed a terrible sight. Blood spurted everywhere.

Megalosaurus —————————

48

LIVED: Late Jurassic times
SIZE: 30ft (9m) long
WEIGHT: 1 ton
DISCOVERED: 1824, in England

OTHER DATA: Bipedal; carnivore; powerful jaws; sharp teeth; short arms; toe and finger claws
NAME MEANS: "Great lizard"

But, then, violence like this was only too common in the prehistoric world. The poor herbivore now bellowed in pain and keeled over. One more bite from Megalosaurus and its victim collapsed dying.

Before the day was out, Megalosaurus would have eaten its fill. Cetiosaurus would be no more than a skeleton, perhaps then slowly becoming fossilized and eventually to be discovered millions of years later.

Cetiosaurus

DINO FACT

Gasosaurus, named after the gas industry and dug up in China, was a relative of gigantic Megalosaurus, and had curved fangs.

MEGASKELETON

No single complete Megalosaurus skeleton has yet been found, but its bones have been unearthed in many parts of Europe. It was in fact the first dinosaur ever to be identified.

Its body, meanwhile, was neatly counterbalanced by a long, thick tail. This was held straight out behind its body as Megalosaurus stalked the Late Jurassic landscape.

Megalosaurus' legs were long and sturdy, adequately supporting its body weight of around one ton.

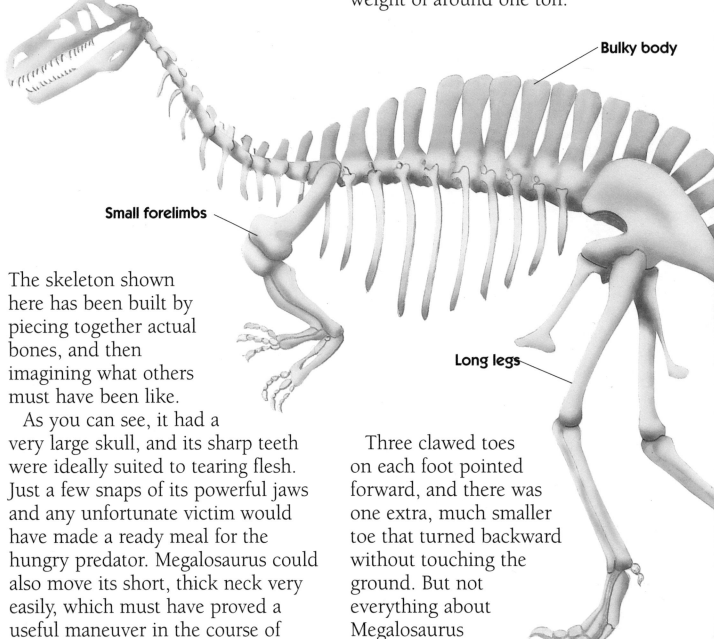

Bulky body

Small forelimbs

Long legs

The skeleton shown here has been built by piecing together actual bones, and then imagining what others must have been like.

As you can see, it had a very large skull, and its sharp teeth were ideally suited to tearing flesh. Just a few snaps of its powerful jaws and any unfortunate victim would have made a ready meal for the hungry predator. Megalosaurus could also move its short, thick neck very easily, which must have proved a useful maneuver in the course of attacking its prey.

Three clawed toes on each foot pointed forward, and there was one extra, much smaller toe that turned backward without touching the ground. But not everything about Megalosaurus was mega!

50

Its two forelimbs were short, although they, too, ended in three clawed fingers.

TRACKING MEGALOSAURUS

Wonderful tracks of this magnificent meat-eater have been found on the Isle of Purbeck, on the southern coast of Great Britain. It is from these, and also from the length of its back legs, that scientists have been able to assess the likely weight and speed of this creature. At one time, scientists thought that Megalosaurus must have been a creature that spent its life traveling about on all-fours. The tracks found by paleontologists have confirmed, however, that this dinosaur was bipedal and never used its arms for walking.

DINO FACT

Megalosaurus could probably run at about 5mph (8km/h) if chasing prey, so it might well also have been able to catch up with *you!*

You can find out how a Megalosaurus bone was originally discovered before the existence of dinosaurs was even known, and how it was thought to be from an elephant or even a giant human being, if you turn to page 168. Only many years later was this bone recognized as part of the remains of a dinosaur.

Lengthy tail

World of Megalosaurus

- First described and named by the scientist and clergyman William Buckland in 1824, a Megalosaurus jawbone is on display at Oxford University Museum, England.

- Megalosaurus' victims might well have included the plant-eater Camptosaurus (CAMP-TOE-<u>SAW</u>-RUS), which also roamed what is now western Europe in Jurassic times.

Ornitholestes

Small and carnivorous, Ornitholestes lived in packs that probably scavenged together. Their diet also consisted of insects and other small creatures, and very early species of birds, possibly. They may have enjoyed eggs, too, as their name, meaning "bird robber," clearly suggests.

One of the dinosaurs inhabiting that part of the planet now known as North America in Late Jurassic times – around 150 million years ago – was Ornitholestes. It was a slim, small dinosaur and measured only about 6.5ft (2m) from the end of its snout to the tip of its tail when fully grown.

MINI CARNIVORE

By dinosaur standards, it was no monster, but it was still a carnivore. Scientists can tell this from the powerful jaws and sharp, strong teeth of its fossilized remains. When Ornitholestes was first discovered, it was given a name meaning "bird robber." Remains found near its skeleton showed that it probably ate many different sorts of small creatures.

But Ornitholestes obviously had hands that were very well-suited to gripping. This would have helped it to pick up round objects – a meal of eggs, perhaps.

Ornitholestes may also have been able to catch early types of birds and make an enjoyable meal of them. They may have scavenged, too. These little carnivores therefore had plenty of choice for the daily menu.

Even so, its head was small for a meat-eater. Odd, too, was the tiny bump or crest that rose just above its nostrils. No one is quite sure whether both male and female Ornitholestes had such a bump. We can only try to guess.

World of Ornitholestes

- Ornitholestes may have eaten small creatures such as lizards or shrews. It would have taken quite a few of these to satisfy an Ornitholestes' appetite.

- Ornitholestes was first discovered in Bone Cabin Quarry, Wyoming, USA, in 1903, together with the fossilized remains of many other dinosaurs.

LIVED: Late Jurassic times
SIZE: 6.5ft (2m) long
WEIGHT: 13kg (29lb)
DISCOVERED: 1903, in USA

OTHER DATA: Bipedal; carnivore; very speedy; powerful jaws; sharp, strong teeth; bump above nostrils; grasping thumbs
NAME MEANS: "Bird robber"

SLENDER SKELETON

Although few remains of this predator have been found – the bones of smaller dinosaurs tended to break up and disintegrate very easily after death – we do know that Ornitholestes had a skeleton that was very much like that of other coelurosaurs (SEA-LURE-OH-SAWS), the family to which this Late Jurassic dinosaur belonged. All had slender bodies, fairly long necks, slim legs, and three-toed feet.

LIZARD-HIPPED

Coelurosaurs had three bones in their hips, each pointing in a different direction. Experts therefore refer to them as being "lizard-hipped" or saurischians (SAW-RISK-EE-ANS). Their pelvis was like that of today's crocodiles, and the pubis bone – as you can see in this reconstruction – thrust downward and forward. In another sort of dinosaur – the ornithischians (ORN-ITH-ISK-EANS) or "bird-hipped" type – two of these bones were parallel, pointing the same way.

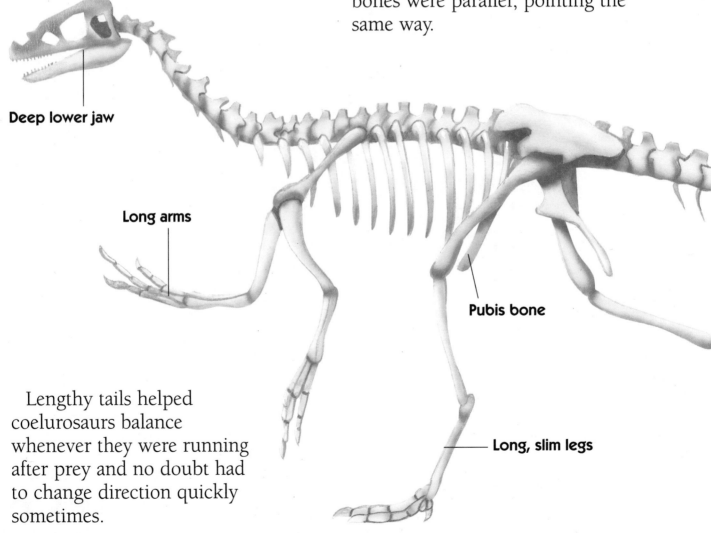

Deep lower jaw

Long arms

Pubis bone

Long, slim legs

Lengthy tails helped coelurosaurs balance whenever they were running after prey and no doubt had to change direction quickly sometimes.

No one is quite sure why some dinosaurs had one type of hip and some, another. It may be that the smaller, swifter dinosaurs had a bigger stride and developed a suitable hip structure that permitted rapid movement in comfort.

SPOT THE DIFFERENCE!

Members of the coelurosaur family were so much alike that even scientists confused their skeletons in the past. Then, in 1980, almost 80 years since the bones of Ornitholestes had first been discovered, it was noticed that it had certain features that distinguished it from all the others in the coelurosaur family. Firstly, its head was particularly small. It also had longer arms than its relatives.

Its hands were rather special, too. On each, it had two very long, clawed fingers of approximately equal length and a shorter thumb that could bend inward like yours and so was very useful for grasping prey.

It had more teeth than other coelurosaurs and so probably a more powerful bite. Its lower jaw was strong and deep; and it had a flexible neck, permitting easy access to any smaller victim, which it would kill by puncturing its flesh with razor-sharp teeth. But Ornitholestes, too, may sometimes have fallen victim to a larger predator looking for an easy meal. Meanwhile, some experts have even suggested that, because it was so small, Ornitholestes may have scavenged at times, perhaps dashing under the legs of larger carnivores and grabbing at their meal, without them noticing at all.

Slim, tapering tail

DINO FACT

It was John Ostrom of Yale University, USA, who first pointed out how Ornitholestes differed from other coelurosaurs.

Ornitholestes is, in fact, the only small theropod of which good remains have been found in the Morrison Formation of the Rocky Mountain states of North America.

Stegosaurus

Discovered in North America, Stegosaurus was a large and rather strange-looking herbivore. The magnificent double row of plates along its back, ending in a spiked tail, puzzled paleontologists for quite a long time. What use, they wondered, could these have had?

About 30ft (9m) long and with thick stumpy legs, Stegosaurus got its name, meaning "roof lizard," because scientists first thought that the plates on its back lay flat, like roof tiles. Today, however, it is widely recognized that they stood up or that they were perhaps adjustable in some way.

They formed a double row right along Stegosaurus' back, but were not directly opposite each other, and possibly functioned as a temperature control so that Stegosaurus was never uncomfortably hot nor too cold. Thus on cool mornings, Stegosaurus may have held its plates to the sun to collect warmth, much as today's solar panels gather heat. But in the middle of the day, Stegosaurus may have turned them sideways, using the breeze to cool down a little.

AMAZING PLATES

Blood vessels ran through these plates which worked rather like a central heating system. No one is yet sure, however, why some dinosaurs needed these "radiators" and some did not.

Large, leaf-shaped plates

World of Stegosaurus

- Although Stegosaurus was quite a frightening size, at times it still needed to defend itself against such fierce, meat-eating monsters as Allosaurus.

LIVED: Late Jurassic times	OTHER DATA: Quadrupedal; herbivore; small head;
SIZE: 30ft (9m) long	tiny brain; plated back; spiked tail;
WEIGHT: 6-8 tons	toothless beak; small cheek teeth
DISCOVERED: 1877, in USA	NAME MEANS: "Roof lizard"

But there may also have been another use for the plates. Some scientists suggest that they might have been brightly colored in the males, who used them to attract females at the beginning of the mating season.

The plates were smallest at the neck and tail ends, and behind them were two pairs of bony spikes, perfect for self-defense against predators whenever danger threatened.

SMALL BRAINED

Stegosaurus had a tiny head for its body size.

Indeed, its skull was only about the size of a large dog's today. At its mouth was a toothless beak made of horn and used for chopping off the leaves on which this herbivore fed.

Its brain, meanwhile, was the smallest, in comparison with the size of its body, of any of the dinosaurs and only as big as a walnut.

With such a minute brain as this, Stegosaurus would not have been very bright, but probably clever enough for its everyday needs.

SKELETAL SURVEY

As you can see in this illustration of Stegosaurus' skeleton, the bony plates on its back were smaller near its head and tail, becoming larger at the middle.

At the sides of its jaws there were small, weak cheek teeth. Like many herbivores, Stegosaurus probably did not chew its food properly but swallowed stones to grind up its intake in its large stomach.

The claws on all of Stegosaurus' toes were like small hooves and so were no good for fighting but may have been useful for getting a grip on very wet or muddy ground.

ON ALL FOURS

Stegosaurus plodded along on all-fours. But it could probably stand on its back legs to feed from trees.

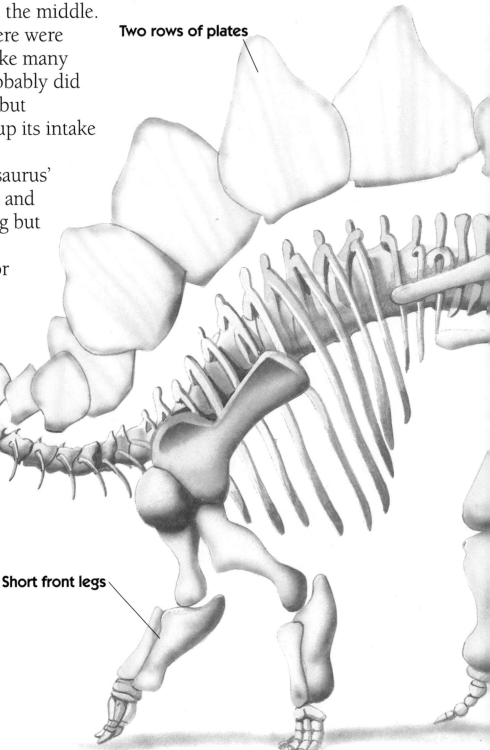

Two rows of plates

Tiny head

Short front legs

DINO FACT

The greatest enemies of Stegosaurus were carnivores, such as the two fearsome giants Allosaurus and Ceratosaurus.

58

Its thick, stumpy legs were clearly designed to support its weight, not for speedy running.

Instead, it would have had to fight for its life, using its very handy tail. Each of the spikes on its tail was up to 3ft (1m) in length and provided a very useful piece of weaponry.

STRANGE SPACE

When Stegosaurus was first discovered, scientists were puzzled by something about its skeleton. What, they wondered, was that space they had noticed at the base of its backbone, near its hips?

Spiked tail

DINO FACT

The two rows of plates running along Stegosaurus' back did not line up symmetrically, but were spaced unevenly.

So, if a hungry carnivore approached, Stegosaurus would not have had much success in escaping its clutches.

Some experts even thought that Stegosaurus might have had another brain there to control its huge body. Later, however, other scientists decided that the hole held lumps of a chemical called *glycogen*. Some animals and birds alive today also have glands that release this chemical. It supplies their muscles with extra energy when they need to fight or run away. Stegosaurus, of course, also needed to call on extra supplies of energy to defend itself against predators.

Vulcanodon

Scientists think that Vulcanodon, an herbivore found without its head, may have been a missing link in the evolution of certain types of dinosaurs.

Everyone was very excited by the discovery of Vulcanodon in Zimbabwe, Africa, in 1972. This was not just another dinosaur which lived in herds, as in this scene, during Early Jurassic times, but possibly a much more interesting creature.

Vulcanodon seemed to belong to the sauropod family – a group of giant plant-eating dinosaurs that lived about 195 million years ago. But it could perhaps have belonged to an earlier family group called the prosauropods, which lived a great deal earlier, between 230 and 195 million years ago. So was it perhaps a missing link?

Vulcanodon was the size of a sauropod, but its hips were like those of a prosauropod – a smaller dinosaur than a sauropod. Experts therefore concluded that Vulcanodon was probably on its way to becoming one of the true sauropods – the largest living creatures ever to have walked on Planet Earth.

DINO FACT

Vulcanodon had one curved claw on the inside of each stumpy foot, which provided a useful defense weapon.

LIVED: Early Jurassic times
SIZE: Perhaps 21ft (6.4m) long
WEIGHT: 3 tons
DISCOVERED: 1972, in Zimbabwe, Africa

OTHER DATA: Herbivore; found without neck or head; bulky body; long tail; thick legs and feet; lived in herds
NAME MEANS: "Volcano tooth"

Probable head

TOOTHY PROBLEM

When a fossilized, headless skeleton of Vulcanodon was originally dug up, scientists found some small, sharp teeth, with edges like steak knives, near by it. At first, they thought that these must have belonged to this new dinosaur and that, therefore, it was a meat-eater. Later, however, they changed their minds, deciding that the teeth must have been from another dinosaur altogether. They had even called the new dinosaur after the teeth.

HEADLESS WONDER

Vulcanodon's missing parts may have been eaten or dragged away by a hungry, scavenging dinosaur after Vulcanodon died. Or perhaps its neck and skull broke off and were washed away in a flood.

What the paleontologists did find, though, was that Vulcanodon had a very strong backbone.

DINO FACT

Vulcanodon's skeleton shows a wide ribcage, which suggests that it had a big stomach to hold all the vegetation it ate.

Missing head and neck

Barrel-like body

(*Vulcanodon* means "volcano tooth.") But Vulcanodon, scientists are now convinced, was actually an herbivore after all, and so is misnamed.

The main problem with the Vulcanodon skeleton, though, was that the head and neck were completely missing. No one knows what had happened to these parts of its body – we can only imagine.

Chunky four-toed feet

World of Vulcanodon

- Vulcanodon males possibly fought with each other over who would mate with the females, but females may actually have led the herds.

- Peaceful, plant-eating Vulcanodon may have lived in herds. They are thought to have gathered to protect all their young if a predator threatened to attack.

Powerful muscles, they guessed, probably supported a long neck. Strangely, they did not find holes in its backbone. Once, scientists thought that large dinosaurs lived some of the time in water.

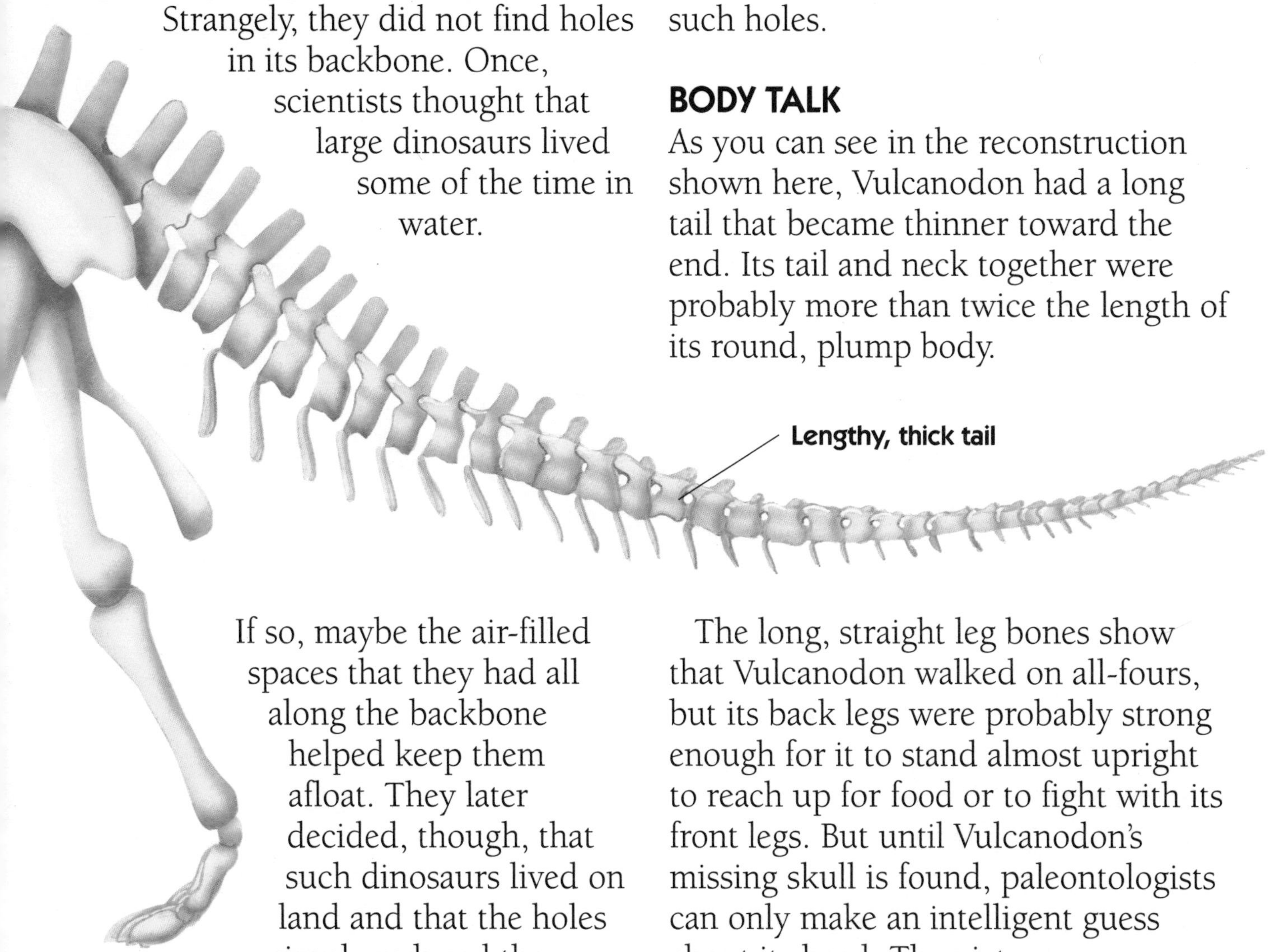

No one knows why such a huge creature as Vulcanodon did not have such holes.

BODY TALK

As you can see in the reconstruction shown here, Vulcanodon had a long tail that became thinner toward the end. Its tail and neck together were probably more than twice the length of its round, plump body.

Lengthy, thick tail

If so, maybe the air-filled spaces that they had all along the backbone helped keep them afloat. They later decided, though, that such dinosaurs lived on land and that the holes simply reduced the weight of their bones.

The long, straight leg bones show that Vulcanodon walked on all-fours, but its back legs were probably strong enough for it to stand almost upright to reach up for food or to fight with its front legs. But until Vulcanodon's missing skull is found, paleontologists can only make an intelligent guess about its head. The picture on pages 60-61 is based on their ideas.

In Cretaceous times

By Cretaceous times, which lasted from 144 to 65 million years ago, when dinosaurs finally became extinct, some of the most well-known dinosaurs of all had evolved – among them T rex, shown centrally in this illustration.

When Planet Earth was home to Tyrannosaurus rex, the weather was much cooler than it had been in previous eras, but there were no very cold winters, even in the far north.

Herds of dinosaurs wandered around in both desert and forest areas in search of food. Plant-eating dinosaurs, such as Euoplocephalus (YOO-OH-PLOH-CEF-AL-US), *below*, with its large tail club and well-armored body, small teeth and weak jaws, grazed on ground ferns and, with other herbivores, nibbled on the very first oak and magnolia trees.

MARINE LIFE

Crocodiles, turtles and fish swam in shallow rivers, while long-necked reptiles, known as plesiosaurs, lived in the seas. In the salty river mouths lurked the huge mosasaurs, about the length of a bus. Dragonflies and other insects buzzed in the air; beetles, crickets and cockroaches crawled in the mosses; and snakes slithered through the ferns. Great pterosaurs flew in the skies.

The very largest plant-eating dinosaurs, such as Brachiosaurus, had died out by this time, but smaller ones took their place.

Giant meat-eaters, such as T rex, hunted them down. Some of them, however, had well-armored bodies and even tail clubs to ward off attackers who thought they would make a good meal.

If a hungry predator caught them, they would try to defend themselves against its mighty jaws.

DIVERSE SPECIES

By this time, much of the land on Planet Earth had broken away to form continents almost as we know them today, so that various parts of the world seem to have become home to particular species of dinosaurs. Protoceratops and Velociraptor, for example, have only been unearthed in China, Mongolia and Russia.

Spinosaurus seems to have been confined to Africa; three-horned Triceratops and long-crested Parasaurolophus to North America. Parts of Asia and what is now the United States, however, may still have been joined because remains of Tyrannosaurus rex have been found in both these regions. But, of course, it could be that remains of any or all of these are as yet undiscovered elsewhere.

BIRD-LIKE DINOSAURS

Toothless, bird-like dinosaurs also appeared during Cretaceous times – long-legged, beaked Gallimimus, for instance, which has been unearthed in Mongolia, and parrot-like Psittacosaurus, discovered in Mongolia, too, as well as China and eastern Europe. You will come face-to-face with all these fascinating creatures, and very many more, throughout the following pages.

Ankylosaurus

Sometimes described as a living tank because of its exceedingly tough body armor, Ankylosaurus would always try to withstand an attack from even the most ferocious of hungry predators.

Ankylosaurus was certainly strongly-built and had superb body-armor that ran all along the top of its torso and right down its tail. This armor was made from many small bony pieces or nodules that were set into Ankylosaurus' skin. Each nodule also had a raised, knobbly portion in the center for additional protection. The nodules were covered with horny scales and fused together (or joined) in bands – which is one reason why this dinosaur was given the name Ankylosaurus, meaning "fused reptile."

   All this body armor was very heavy, just as you might expect.

LIVED: Late Cretaceous times	**OTHER DATA:** Quadrupedal; herbivore;
SIZE: 20ft (6m) long	spined body; tail club; beak; sturdy
WEIGHT: 2 tons	legs; soft belly
DISCOVERED: 1908, in Canada	**NAME MEANS:** "Fused reptile"

In fact, Ankylosaurus weighed over two tons – almost half as much as an African elephant. It was long, too – nearly the length of a bus.

SOFT-BELLIED

Hard, sharp spines sticking out from its back made this armor even more impenetrable, so that the only spot on Ankylosaurus' body that was not adequately protected from a predator was the soft underbelly. Enemies could sometimes take advantage of this by pushing Ankylosaurus on to its back and then attacking this highly vulnerable area.

But, most of the time, the prospect of trying to find a way through Ankylosaurus' armor-plated body would have been too much for predators. Even the most vicious meat-eating dinosaurs, such as Tyrannosaurus rex, should have thought twice before daring to launch an attack. As you can see in this illustration, although rather smaller, the armored Ankylosaurus could easily give its enemy a mighty whack with its enormous tail club. Bipedal Tyrannosaurus might then have toppled over. It was not nearly as stable on its two legs as Ankylosaurus was on all-fours. After such a blow, it would have been unlikely to pick itself up, and so probably suffered a slow and agonizing death.

67

CLUBBED TAIL WEAPON

The most spectacular part of Ankylosaurus' large, tough skeleton was, of course, the bulky club at the end of its thick, sturdy tail. This mighty weapon, used for self-defense, was about five times wider than *your* head and made from chunks of solid bone which were fused together completely at one side.

Nevertheless, Ankylosaurus was an herbivore and so never attacked for meat. Rather, it used its toothless beak for nipping leaves off branches. Its teeth were farther back in its mouth and quite small and weak, but they were adequate for chewing soft plants. Ankylosaurus also had a bony shelf between its nose and mouth, allowing it to chew and breathe at the same time. Human beings can do this, but most of today's reptiles cannot.

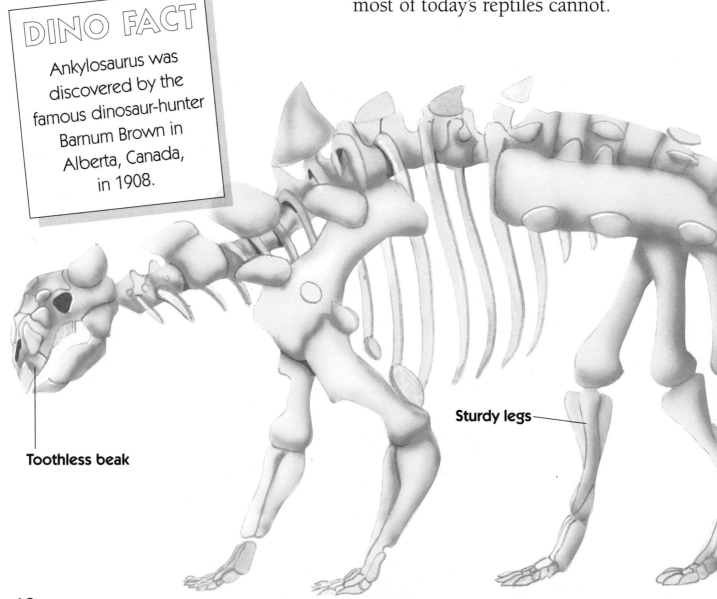

DINO FACT

Ankylosaurus was discovered by the famous dinosaur-hunter Barnum Brown in Alberta, Canada, in 1908.

Toothless beak

Sturdy legs

World of Ankylosaurus

- Ankylosaurids, the family to which Ankylosaurus belonged, were known to have had a tail club which could be swung from side to side and used as a mighty weapon.

- Euoplocephalus was an armored cousin of Ankylosaurus, very much like it but somewhat smaller. It, too, lived in what is now Alberta, Canada, and perhaps also China.

Ankylosaurus' skull was broad and covered with chunks of bone. Small horns also stood at the four corners of the skull. The creature's jaws, too, were protected by slabs of bone. Ankylosaurus' head was certainly well-protected – it even had bony eyelids.

Ankylosaurus stood on four strong legs, supporting the heavy armor plating of its body. Surprisingly, experts have calculated that it was not necessarily a slow and lumbering creature.

On the contrary, it could move reasonably quickly by taking long strides. If, however, it found itself right up against a predator and was therefore unable to run away, there was another strategy it could adopt. It would bend its legs and dig its foot claws deep into the ground to protect its soft belly in case an attacker tried to topple it over.

The numerous bony plates and spines on Ankylosaurus' back and tail were not truly part of its skeleton. They were embedded in its skin, not attached to its spine or ribs, and so cannot be seen on this skeletal reconstruction. Nevertheless they were a most important part of an Ankylosaurus' body structure.

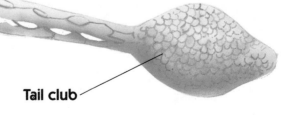

Tail club

Baryonyx

No wonder this British dinosaur has earned itself the nickname "Claws." The enormous claws at the end of the thumbs on its forelimbs were about the length of *your* entire arm!

Imagine a scene, like the one *below*, around 120 million years ago in the area we now know as England. These were Early Cretaceous times, when there were many rivers and lakes, surrounded by rich vegetation.

Here, Baryonyx – a carnivore – would feed on a wide variety of small creatures. But, most unusual for a dinosaur, there is evidence that it also went fishing, as you can see here.

Nose bump

Huge thumb claw

LIVED: Early Cretaceous times
SIZE: 30ft (9m) long
WEIGHT: 2 tons
DISCOVERED: 1983, in England

OTHER DATA: Carnivore; large thumb claws; weak teeth; caught and ate fish; crocodile-like jaws; sturdy limbs; bump on snout
NAME MEANS: "Heavy claw"

World of Baryonyx

- Similar bones found in West Africa indicate that Baryonyx may have lived in that part of the world, too, as well as in what is now mainland Europe, when this was all one landmass.

- Dinosaurs that roamed what is now England alongside Baryonyx included Altispinax (AL-TEA-SPEEN-AX), Iguanodon, and Hypsilophodon, as well as Astrodon (AS-TROH-DON), a large plant-eater.

That is where its enormous thumb claws came in handy. Scientists know that Baryonyx ate fish because fossilized fish scales were found in its remains.

BARYONYX'S BONES

When paleontologists first dug up Baryonyx's remains, they found them right next to the fossilized bones of an Iguanodon – another dinosaur with a weapon on its thumbs.

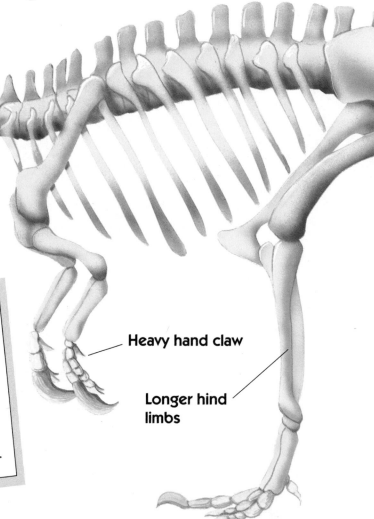

Nose bump

Crocodile-like jaws

Could it be that the two creatures perished, scientists wonder, in the course of a fight over food or territory?

From the skeleton of Baryonyx that experts have managed to piece together, what we do know for sure – as shown in the reconstruction illustrated here – is that Baryonyx had a number of fairly distinctive body parts. Its elongated skull, for instance, was supported by a long neck.

At 30ft (9m) in length, Baryonyx was as long as a bus, and heavy, too, weighing in at about 2 tons – the equivalent of about twenty five of today's fully-grown, average-sized men!

FIRM FOOTING

Its back legs were sturdy, and the front limbs quite powerful, too. Some scientists even think that Baryonyx may have been able to move around on all-fours like a quadruped, perhaps when prowling near a river, waiting for signs of fish.

Heavy hand claw

Longer hind limbs

DINO FACT

Baryonyx's remains are among the best preserved of any of the dinosaurs that roamed our planet in Early Cretaceous times.

Oddly, Baryonyx had about twice as many teeth in its crocodile-like jaws as most meat-eaters. Largest at the front and decreasing in size toward the back of its mouth, these teeth were shaped like cones and slightly serrated – such teeth were ideal, in fact, for grasping at slithery, wriggling victims like fish, or smaller dinosaurs, such as Hypsilophodon, or even a young Iguanodon.

Now take a look at Baryonyx's tail which was almost as long as the rest of its body and tapered toward the tip.

Scientists have concluded that Baryonyx's great claws are unlikely to have been on its back feet. It would have been far too heavy to stand on one hind leg and then slash with the claw on the other leg, as a very much lighter and smaller dinosaur like Deinonychus could easily do. Baryonyx's front limbs, however, were perfectly strong enough to carry these magnificent weapons. What wonderful tools they must have made for Baryonyx to catch a seafood dinner!

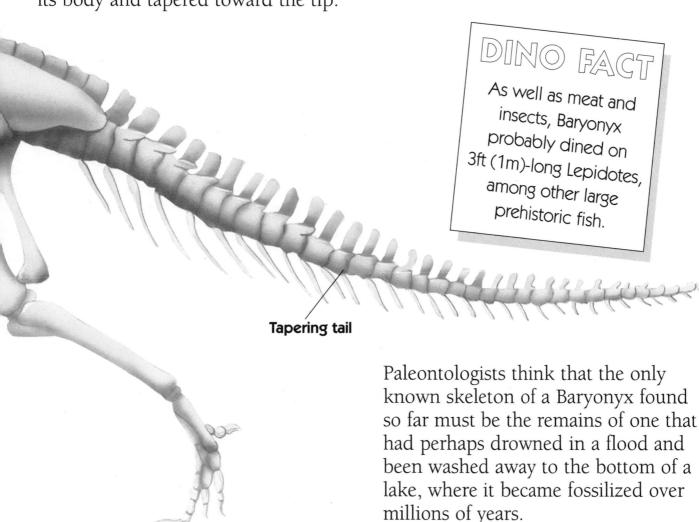

DINO FACT

As well as meat and insects, Baryonyx probably dined on 3ft (1m)-long Lepidotes, among other large prehistoric fish.

Tapering tail

Paleontologists think that the only known skeleton of a Baryonyx found so far must be the remains of one that had perhaps drowned in a flood and been washed away to the bottom of a lake, where it became fossilized over millions of years.

Carnotaurus

Two bumpy-skinned dinosaurs engage in battle. One is Titanosaurus, a large herbivore; the other, Carnotaurus, is a fearsome horned predator that will fight to the death for a meal.

An Early Cretaceous dinosaur from around 140 million years ago, Carnotaurus was a theropod. Lots of dinosaurs belonged to this group. Some were huge, some smaller. But they all had certain things in common. First of all, they were all carnivores, with sharp teeth and claws. They also all walked on two legs only and had short arms. There were theropods on Planet Earth from around 220 million years ago, when dinosaurs evolved, to when they finally became extinct, 65 million years ago. But, although it was a theropod, Carnotaurus also had something rather special about it.

BULL-LIKE HORNS
Extraordinary for a dinosaur, Carnotaurus had two small, thick, bull-like horns growing over its two beady eyes.

In fact, it is because of this pair of horns that Carnotaurus was given its name, meaning "meat-eating bull."

Within the great jaws of its squat head were also lots of sharp, slim teeth – ideal for coping with raw meat.

ALL THERE
When the remains of Carnotaurus were first dug up in Argentina, South America, in 1985, experts were delighted, because most of the fossilized bones were there.

World of Carnotaurus

- No one knows for sure what dinosaurs smelled like, but it is easy to imagine! They did not enter water that much, and many were far too big ever to lick themselves clean.

- Carnotaurus belonged to a family called the Abelisaurids (AB-EL-EE-SAW-RIDS), all predatory. Some lived alongside Carnotaurus, among them Abelisaurus and Noasaurus (NO-A-SAW-RUS).

LIVED: Early Cretaceous times
SIZE: 25ft (7.5m) long
WEIGHT: 1 ton
DISCOVERED: 1985, in Argentina

OTHER DATA: Bipedal; carnivore; bumpy skin; two small horns; long tail; heavy; sharp teeth
NAME MEANS: "Meat-eating bull"

Carnotaurus

Titanosaurus

This meant that they could reconstruct it fairly accurately. They were even able to estimate that its total weight, when alive and covered with flesh and skin, would probably have been about 12 times heavier than today's average man. That certainly shows that Carnotaurus was a monster to be marveled at.

75

CAMOUFLAGE

In his book *The Lost World* (the sequel to *Jurassic Park*), Michael Crichton describes the frightening moment when one of his heroes suddenly catches sight of two large dinosaurs, staring intently at him.

Until then, the dinosaurs had been invisible, the coloring of their bodies blending in perfectly with the leaves surrounding them. (If you dressed all in green, and crawled through some green bushes, you would be perfectly camouflaged, too.)

LIKE A CHAMELEON

In Crichton's imagination, these Carnotaurus could change the color of their skin – and its patterns – in order to "disappear" amidst their surroundings, even more skillfully than chameleons.

No one is sure about the coloring of Carnotaurus' skin, nor whether it could in fact change it. Nevertheless, Michael Crichton's fantasy about this could well have been true. Indeed, it is likely that some dinosaurs were able to camouflage themselves among the vegetation of prehistoric times, all the better to hide and then spring out on a victim. The Carnotaurus in this illustration, as you can see, has changed its color from that on the previous page to blend in with the landscape.

DINO FACT

Carnotaurus' home, South America, was a separate landmass back in Cretaceous times and distinct species evolved there.

76

Chasmosaurus

When two Chasmosaurus confronted each other face-to-face, there was sure to be a battle. The others in the herd would prepare to witness a spectacular Cretaceous scene.

One of a group of dinosaurs known as the *ceratopsids*, Chasmosaurus is easily recognizable because of its distinctive head frill. The larger a male's frill, the more it would impress other Chasmosaurus in the herd.

During most of the year, herds of Chasmosaurus lived peacefully together, grazing across their territory and looking after their young. But when the mating season came around, the large adult males went to war, fighting each other to see who would mate with the females.

TEST OF STRENGTH

Two male Chasmosaurus would challenge one another, as you can see in this illustration, roaring and pawing at the ground with their front feet. They may also have raised their huge neck frills in a display of size and strength to frighten off the smaller, weaker male.

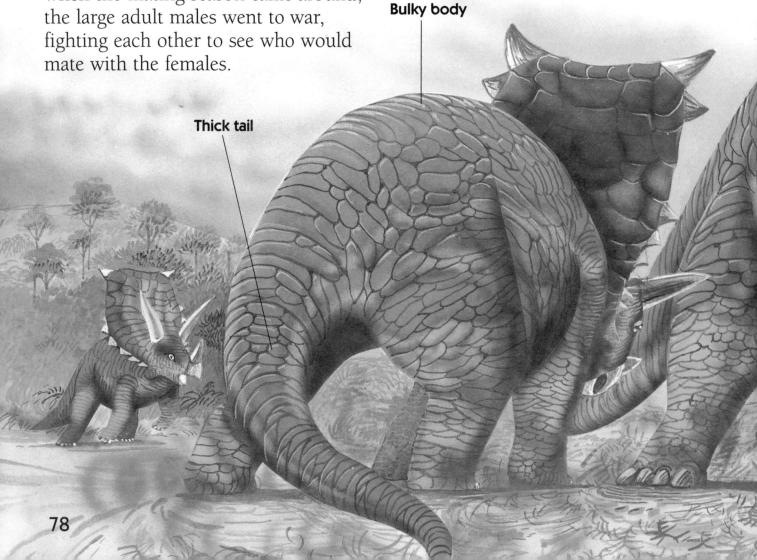

Bulky body

Thick tail

78

LIVED: Late Cretaceous times
SIZE: 17ft (5.2m) long
WEIGHT: 2-5 tons
DISCOVERED: 1902, in Canada

OTHER DATA: Herbivore; large neck frill, edged with spikes; horny beak; two brow horns; nose horn
NAME MEANS: "Cleft lizard"

The two Chasmosaurus would now charge, trying to stab at each other with their long horns. Turning, they may then have lashed their tails. One hard blow might have been enough to break the opponent's leg.

FIGHTING OVER FEMALES

As the rest of the herd watched, this battle would fill the air with dust and the smell of crushed plants. But the encounter seldom ended in death. The two males were only trying to prove which was the stronger. The victor would then mate with his pick of the females.

Spiky-edge to large head frill

Sharp beak

FRILLED SKELETON

Chasmosaurus had a very strong skeleton to support its heavy body and a magnificent neck frill. But it was not built for speed. So although it had a powerful set of muscles to move its stumpy front and back legs, it usually plodded along slowly.

Huge amounts of food were necessary to keep Chasmosaurus healthy and to satisfy its appetite. The size of its ribs points to a big stomach.

In its thick neck and around its strong backbone, Chasmosaurus had powerful muscles to hold up the weight of its long head and magnificent neck frill.

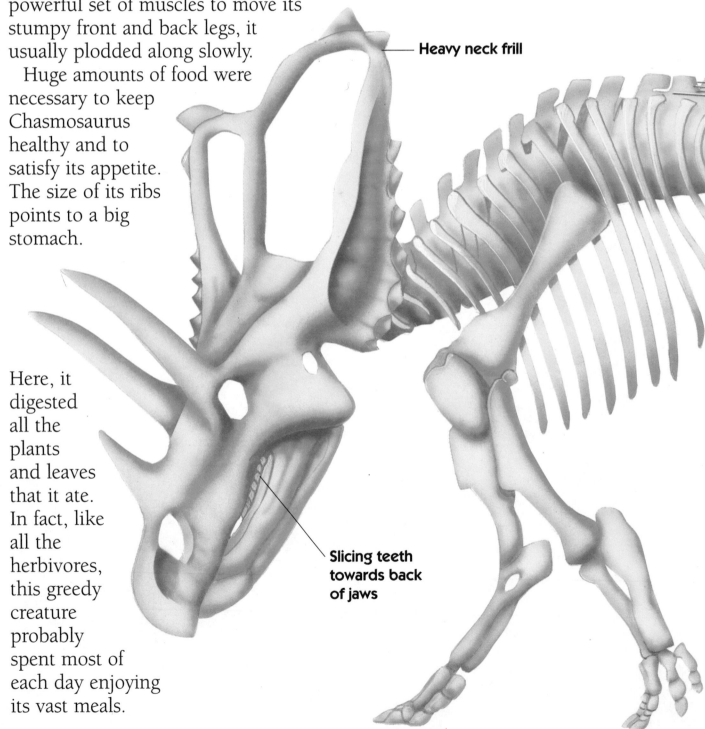

Heavy neck frill

Slicing teeth towards back of jaws

Here, it digested all the plants and leaves that it ate. In fact, like all the herbivores, this greedy creature probably spent most of each day enjoying its vast meals.

80

World of Chasmosaurus

- Other frilled dinosaurs from North America include Monoclonius (MON-OH-<u>KLONE</u>-EE-US), found in Montana about 150 years ago and with a single nose horn.

- Styracosaurus (STY-RACK-OH-<u>SAW</u>-RUS), a heavily built plant-eater found in the same region, had a single nose horn, too, but a frill with six long spikes jutting out from it.

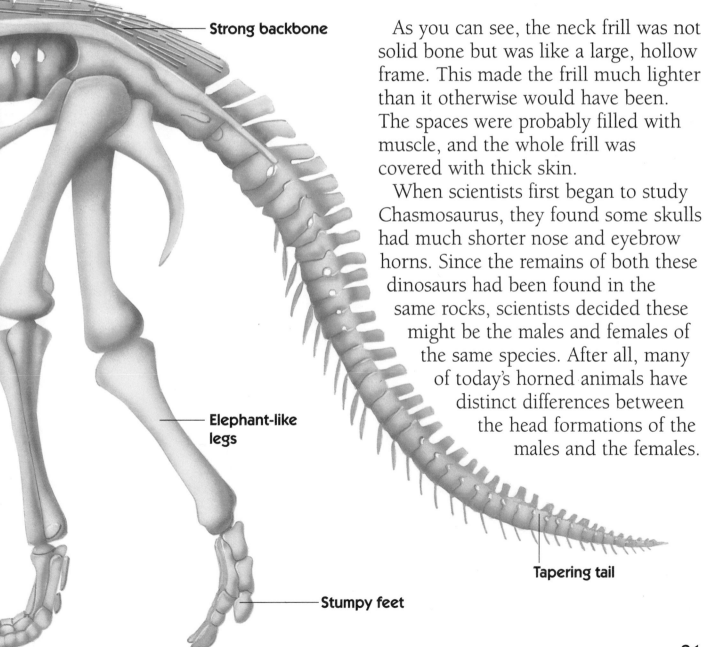

Strong backbone

Elephant-like legs

Stumpy feet

Tapering tail

As you can see, the neck frill was not solid bone but was like a large, hollow frame. This made the frill much lighter than it otherwise would have been. The spaces were probably filled with muscle, and the whole frill was covered with thick skin.

When scientists first began to study Chasmosaurus, they found some skulls had much shorter nose and eyebrow horns. Since the remains of both these dinosaurs had been found in the same rocks, scientists decided these might be the males and females of the same species. After all, many of today's horned animals have distinct differences between the head formations of the males and the females.

Deinonychus

Few dinosaurs were so well-equipped as Deinonychus for killing with a dreaded sickle-shaped claw on the second toe of each of its feet.

Growing to about 5in (13cm) in length, Deinonychus sickle claws were not only huge but were also specially designed weapons, used to slash victims. In fact, they were so big that, when Deinonychus walked along, it probably used its muscles to hold them off the ground in order to keep them sharp.

As soon as it had caught up with its prey, a single Deinonychus would have leaped on to the victim's back, clamped its jaws around the animal's neck and then, using the huge sickle claws on its feet, ripped open its prey.

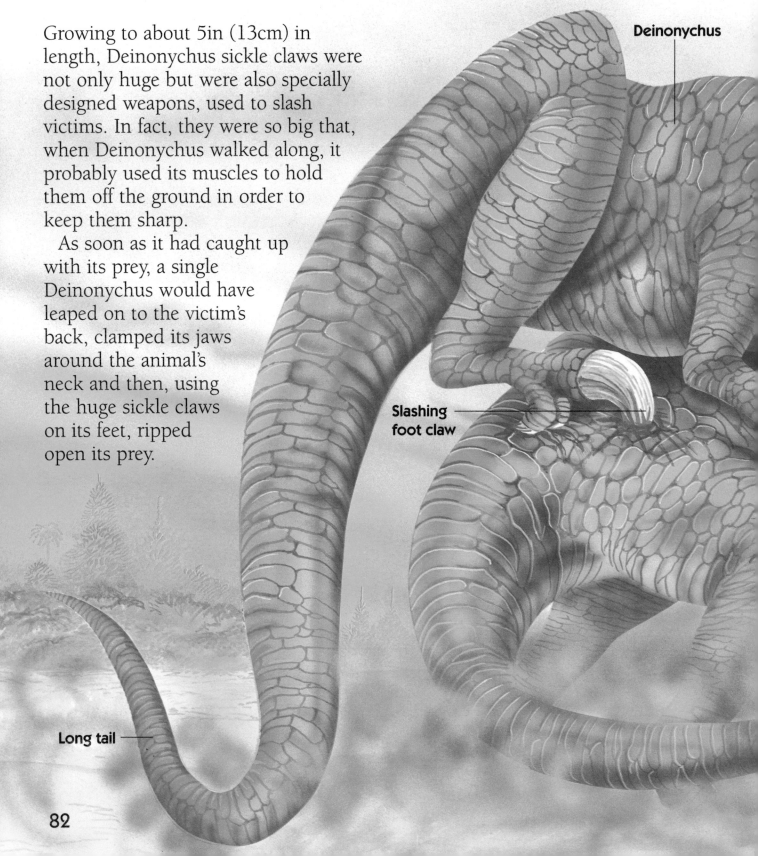

Deinonychus

Slashing foot claw

Long tail

LIVED: Early Cretaceous times
SIZE: 10ft (3m) long
WEIGHT: 155lb (70kg)
DISCOVERED: 1964, USA

OTHER DATA: Carnivore; large clawed hands; huge sickle claw on each foot; long tail; sharp teeth; low head; big jaws
NAME MEANS: "Terrible claw"

A victim, such as the Zephyrosaurus (ZEF-EYE-ROE-<u>SAW</u>-RUS), shown here, would have died in agony.

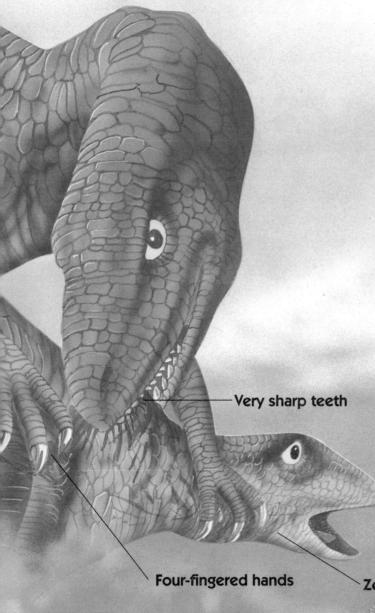

Very sharp teeth

Four-fingered hands

Zephyrosaurus

PACK OF THREE

When Deinonychus' bones were first dug up, scientists found that they came from three Deinonychus skeletons lying close to each other. Nearby, scientists also found the skeleton of a large plant-eater, Tenontosaurus (TEN-<u>ON</u>-TOE-<u>SAW</u>-RUS).

The three Deinonychus must have been hunting in a pack and, greedy for a meal, might have decided to attack the giant Tenontosaurus together.

This plant-eater was far bigger than a Deinonychus – so one alone could never have killed it. But by working together, the three Deinonychus could have brought the larger animal down, leaping on to it all at once and then tearing at it with their vicious claws.

If the Tenontosaurus had tried to run away, one Deinonychus might have grabbed the animal's tail and back legs to slow it down. The others, meanwhile, would probably have clung to its neck, chest and belly, kicking with their clawed hind feet to wound and kill their huge prey.

83

A HUNTER'S SKELETON

Scientists have now put together a great deal of information about Deinonychus, from the several hundred bones that were first dug up from a hillside in the state of Montana, USA, in 1964.

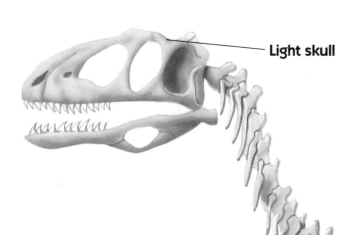

— Light skull

The skeletal remains were discovered by an American paleontologist, named John Ostrom, together with Grant E. Meyer, and their team.

Three things stand out if you look at the reconstruction of Deinonychus' skeleton shown here – its strong jaws, long arms and dreadful foot claws.

LIGHTWEIGHT HEAD

Deinonychus' skull was large and filled with holes (known as "windows") which made it lightweight. There were big openings for its eyes, and plenty of space for the strong jaw muscles, which must have given Deinonychus a very powerful bite.

The backward-curving teeth helped Deinonychus tear off meat from its victim. The more a victim struggled to get free, the more those teeth would bite!

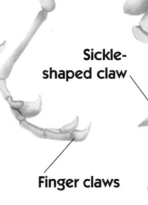

Sickle-shaped claw

Finger claws

DINO FACT

Scientists have come to the conclusion that those dinosaurs with big eyes may have been active at night as well as during the day.

STRONG-ARMED DINOSAUR

Deinonychus had a supple neck. Notice, too, how the bones of its arms are almost as thick as its leg bones. This means that its arms must have been quite powerful.

But its feet were, of course, its main weapon, and were used to slash and kill as it held its prey at arm's length.

TAIL END

The last part of the tail was stiffened with bony rods that enabled Deinonychus to hold it level when running at high speed and so maintain its balance. One flick of the tail, and Deinonychus could change its direction rapidly – a useful trick when chasing after the next meal.

There are a few skeletons of Deinonychus on display at the American Museum of Natural History in New York, USA. This dinosaur's bones can also be seen at another American museum, the Peabody Museum of Natural History, Yale University, New Haven, Connecticut. Some remains found in Japan are also thought to be from a Deinonychus-like dinosaur.

THREE-FINGERED HANDS

The remains show that Deinonychus had three big, strong fingers on each of its hands. Each finger carried a mean-looking, sharply curved claw which could do a lot of damage when raked over a victim's skin – but not nearly so much, of course, as the far larger and crueler switchblades on both its feet.

Stiff, tapering tail

World of Deinonychus

- Scientists think Deinonychus may often have held its unfortunate victims at a distance in order to kick at them violently with its terrible claws.

- Deinonychus had masses of very sharp teeth, just like steak knives. They curved slightly backwards and helped give Deinonychus a tight grip on its prey.

Gallimimus

Often described as an ostrich-like dinosaur, but bigger by far than today's ostriches, Gallimimus certainly had the skeleton of a champion runner with long, slim but strong legs, and lengthy, slender foot bones.

There are a number of features that make it easy to identify a Gallimimus. Firstly, its two back legs were long and thin – clearly ideal for taking great strides. In fact, if you have ever watched an ostrich on the run, you will have a good idea of how fast a Gallimimus may have sprinted. At the end of its long legs, Gallimimus also had lengthy foot bones, making scientists even more certain that it could run at a fantastic rate.

Most of the time, therefore, this ace sprinter would have been able to escape from any threatening predators with considerable ease, probably outrunning them in no time. No doubt its considerable speed also helped it catch lots of small prey, such as the dragonfly in the picture, *below*. Otherwise, it probably ate mostly leaves and berries, as well as any lizards and shrews that it chanced upon.

S-shaped neck

Toothless beak

Long, slim legs

Stiff tail

LIVED: Late Cretaceous times	**OTHER DATA:** Bipedal; omnivore; ostrich-like;
SIZE: 20ft (6m) long	toothless beak; long, slim legs,
WEIGHT: 968lb (440kg)	S-shaped neck
DISCOVERED: 1963, in Mongolia	**NAME MEANS:** "Fowl mimic"

FEEDING TIME

Gallimimus had no teeth in its beak. It therefore probably ate anything that was small and soft enough to swallow without having to bother about chewing. So its diet may well have included eggs belonging to other dinosaurs – it could have cracked them open with its sharp beak – as well as plants, lizards, insects and other small creatures.

It could be that Gallimimus used its claws to scratch at the soil in an attempt to uncover tasty worms and roots; and it probably also used its claws to hold small prey.

One thing is certain: Gallimimus must have gotten all it needed to eat to give it the strength to run like the wind.

Small forearms

87

SPEEDY RUNNERS

Picture the scene. Like lightning, dozens of Gallimimus are dashing across the plain at a rate of almost 25mph (40km/h). (That's about the speed limit in most towns today.) Even if *you* ran *your* fastest, you would never be able to run so quickly. Perhaps you have seen the movie *Jurassic Park* and remember the incredible shots of a herd of computer-generated Gallimimus stampeding past at a tremendous rate.

The hungry Saurornithoides are intelligent predators with grasping hands and nasty claws on their second toes. And the prospect of a meal of Gallimimus is very inviting to the crafty carnivores.

As the Gallimimus race away in panic and the dust of the Mongolian desert rises in their wake, the frightened creatures hold out their stiff tails behind them. This is to help them balance when racing along, at a speed so tremendous that their legs would barely touch the ground. Their strides are huge, but will they be able to outrun the Saurornithoides?

But why should the Gallimimus in the sequence of images shown here need to run so speedily? Follow the story frame by frame and you will see that a few greedy Saurornithoides (SAW-ROAR-NITH-OID-EEZ) are after them, and the slender Gallimimus are no match.

Fortunately, the gap between the two species grows larger by the minute. The Gallimimus are certainly the faster runners. The chase is very tiring for the smaller Gallimimus, however.

World of Gallimimus

- With its long, slim, flexible, and S-shaped neck, held upright when running, Gallimimus could easily look around to spot an enemy on the prowl.

- Gallimimus belonged to a group of dinosaurs known as ornithomimosaurs (OR-NITH-OH-<u>MIME</u>-OH-SAWS).

- All ornithomimosaurs had slender limbs, big eyes, toothless beaks and were speedy runners.

- Excellent specimens of Gallimimus that have been unearthed seem to indicate that they probably lived near large rivers.

Still young, they find it hard to keep up with the rest of their herd. One young Gallimimus in particular lags behind the predators, who are soon on its tail. Then, suddenly, a giant Tarbosaurus (TAR-BOH-<u>SAW</u>-RUS) announces its presence with a mighty roar. It is also on the prowl for dinner.

So now it is the Saurornithoides' turn to be fearful as the Tarbosaurus leaps out at them. What a lucky escape! For a moment, they forget about the young Gallimimus and it is able to romp away unharmed, returning to the safety of the herd.

Hypsilophodon

Hardly bigger than an adult human being is today, Hypsilophodon was a timid Early Cretaceous herbivore that is likely to have lived in herds.

Many dinosaurs have only been dug up in one part of the world. Remains of Hypsilophodon, however, have been unearthed in lots of different places, showing that its habitat was widespread.

INTERNATIONAL DINOSAUR

In all, the bones from more than twenty different Hypsilophodon skeletons have been found on the Isle of Wight alone, off the southern British coast, where it was first discovered in 1849. However, Hypsilophodon did not live on a small island all those millions of years ago, but roamed across a large land mass which has since split up to become not only islands but also the continents we know today, including North America and Europe. That is why Hypsilophodon remains have also been dug up in Portugal, in southern Europe, as well as South Dakota. in the United States.

In fact, it is likely that bones from this creature are buried in many other places around the world, too. A close relative of Hypsilophodon has even been found in the icy wastes of Antarctica.

In its general appearance, Hypsilophodon is much like Iguanodon, except that it did not have that dinosaur's spiked thumbs and was much smaller.

LIVED: Early Cretaceous times
SIZE: 6.5ft (2m) long
WEIGHT: 112lb (50kg)
DISCOVERED: 1849, on the Isle of Wight

OTHER DATA: Bipedal; herbivore; horny beak; short arms; long legs; cheek pouches; stiff tail
NAME MEANS: "High ridge tooth"

91

BIRD-HIPPED

Hypsilophodon's skeleton was typical of the ornithischian or "bird-hipped" dinosaurs that were all herbivores. As you can see in this illustration, bones in the hip area pointed backward, as they would in birds.

Its feet also had elongated bones, as shown, and as well as helping Hypsilophodon to keep its balance when running, its stiff tail may have been used in moments of panic to swipe against the legs of any threatening predator.

As you can see from the skeleton *below*, the skull of Hypsilophodon was small and pointed.

Ring of bone around eye

Lightweight skull

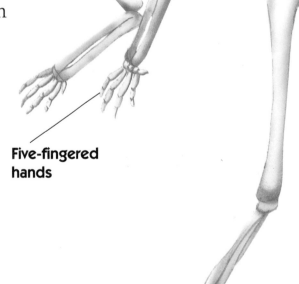

Hypsilophodon had a body that was obviously made for speed. Its leg bones were long and thin, which would have allowed it to move at a fast pace and to take lengthy strides when it was running.

Five-fingered hands

DINO FACT

When Hypsilophodon's bones were first unearthed, they were mistakenly thought to belong to a baby Iguanodon.

World of Hypsilophodon

- Hypsilophodon was likely prey for many large carnivores such as Altispinax. They would therefore have had to run like the wind to escape its gigantic jaws and a cruel fate.

- Experts have suggested that all the Hypsilophodon whose skeletons have been found together on the Isle of Wight may have become trapped in mud or drowned in a sudden flood.

Its skull was probably quite light, too, which would have meant that Hypsilophodon could move its head from side to side very easily to keep a look-out for enemies.

Around each eye, there was a ring of small bones. Lots of reptiles have this, and scientists believe it may be a sign of good eyesight.

SHARP BEAK
With its sharp, horny beak, Hypsilophodon could nip off tough leaves and shoots very easily.

Lengthy stiff tail

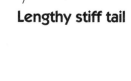

Long foot bones

Behind its beak, Hypsilophodon's cheek teeth were numerous and would have been put to good use for chewing. What was more, this herbivore could use its special cheek pouches to stop its food from falling out the sides of its mouth while it was chewing. It probably therefore needed to feed rather more efficiently than other plant-eaters not endowed with such a facility.

93

Iguanodon

First discovered after Mary Ann Mantell found its teeth in England in 1822 entirely by accident while out walking, Iguanodon remains have also been unearthed in a Belgian coal mine.

From its tracks, we know that Iguanodon lived in herds, all the adults protecting the young when they migrated.

When it was young, Iguanodon may have walked on its back legs only. But as these became heavier, it began to walk on all-fours.

Parrot-like beak

Spiked thumbs

LIVED: Early Cretaceous times
SIZE: 30ft (9m) long
WEIGHT: 5 tons
DISCOVERED: 1822, in England

OTHER DATA: Herbivore; spiked thumbs; mighty tail; self-sharpening beak; cheek teeth; finger hooves; bipedal when young
NAME MEANS: "Iguana tooth"

MAIN FEATURES

Iguanodon's principal characteristics were its spiked thumb weapons and beak. It also had little fingers that could bend very easily – very useful for grasping twigs – and three flat fingers with hooves which bent outward, instead of inward like yours.

Iguanodon probably also had cheek pouches in its mouth, as did certain other herbivores, such as Hypsilophodon.

Heavy tail

Clawed feet

IN SELF-DEFENSE

An account of a typical Cretaceous day illustrates the sort of dangers that an herbivore, even one as large as Iguanodon, had to face and how it could defend itself.

Picture the scene. An Iguanodon herd is browsing among giant ferns. They would have to spend most of their time looking for food, like most big plant-eaters, and are busy chopping off leaves with their sharp beaks.

Shrieking with terror, the herd tries to run away. They can move fairly rapidly – up to 25mph (40km/h). But the carnivore is quick on its feet, too, and soon catches up with one Iguanodon, grabbing at it with its mighty claws and preparing to sink its teeth into the herbivore's throat.

But the Iguanodon knows how to fight back to protect itself and can call on deadly weapons.

Suddenly, a large carnivore springs out of the bushes. This ferocious creature has a large appetite to satisfy and has been stalking the Iguanodon.

These are the thumb spikes that it has on each hand. As it plunges both into the predator's neck, the meat-eater yells out in pain. Again and again, the Iguanodon stabs at the carnivore and it is soon bleeding furiously.

World of Iguanodon

- Iguanodon belonged to a group of dinosaurs that had hips like those of birds, whereas some other dinosaurs had lizard-like hip structures.

- When Iguanodon's bones were first found, scientists made an error and thought they belonged to something like a giant lizard.

At last it gives up and limps away. The ravenous carnivore will have to wait for its meal.

The Iguanodon now returns to the herd and spends the rest of the day resting and eating with its family. One of their number has been lucky and had a narrow escape from death.

It would seem that Iguanodon's spiked thumbs have saved it yet again from ending up as a carnivore's dinner.

97

Maiasaura

A large, gentle herbivore, Maiasaura was given its name, meaning "good mother lizard" because there is evidence that it looked after its young very well while they were still in the nest.

Paleontologists have found a wealth of evidence concerning the nesting habits of Maiasaura. They know, for instance, that their nests were made from mud and sand. Each one was bowl-shaped, about as deep as *you* are tall, and about 6ft (2m) across – that is about the size of a double bed but round instead of oblong.

A mother Maiasaura would line her nest with soft plants and generally laid about twenty eggs in all.

The sun heated the nests by day, and the sand helped keep them at a steady temperature, too. Heat from rotting vegetation in the nests provided warmth as well. A mother Maiasaura may also have curled up around her eggs at night.

The young were only about 14in (35cm) long when they hatched – that's small enough to sit in your bathroom wash-basin. In two months, however, they probably doubled in size.

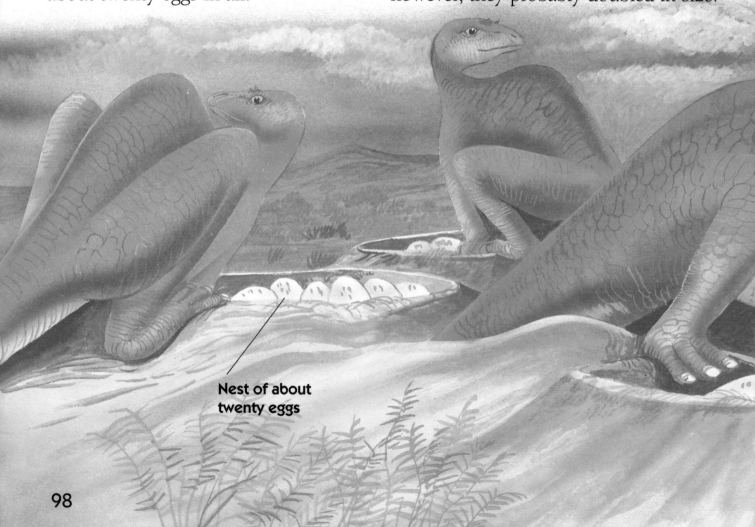

Nest of about twenty eggs

LIVED: Late Cretaceous times
SIZE: 30ft (9m) long
WEIGHT: 6 tons
DISCOVERED: 1978, in USA

OTHER DATA: Herbivore; toothless beak; thick tail; short, bony crest; shallow jaws; lots of cheek teeth; mostly quadrupedal
NAME MEANS: "Good mother lizard"

GOOD MOTHERS

Their mothers looked after them well, and so the hatchlings did not have to use up energy looking for food. Instead, they stayed safely inside the nest while their mothers – and possibly also their fathers – collected leaves and plants for them.

Maiasaura parents were kept very busy. They each had to find as much plant food as a grown human being weighs today, for themselves and for their young, in a single day. The adult Maiasaura would chew up and swallow food where they found it.

They could then regurgitate the food when they returned to the nests, and the young would eat what their parents brought up. Some birds today actually feed their young in this way.

But there were probably disadvantages to being good parents for so long. If, for example, their parents were killed by a meat-eating dinosaur, or died in some other way, the young usually died, too, because they had not learned to fend for themselves yet. In such an instance, they would have been easy prey for any small theropod.

Ridged back

ON THE MOVE

Even when they were not nesting, Maiasaura lived in herds, as many large plant-eating animals do today. We know this because paleontologists have found the bones of tens of thousands of hadrosaurs – probably killed by the poisonous gas and smoke from an erupting volcano – in the same area.

Such large herds could not have stayed in one place for long before all the plants there were eaten.

Bulky body

Long snout

Thick, sturdy legs

Heavy tail

World of Maiasaura

- Maiasaura was a *hadrosaurine* dinosaur, and had a characteristic slight ridge along its head and back.

- Pads under its feet protected it from being damaged by rough ground.

- Maiasaura probably laid eggs each year, just before the rainy season.

- A small space would be left between each egg in the nest so that the babies could hatch easily.

That is why experts believe hadrosaurs probably regularly migrated, moving constantly from one place to another in search of food.

LEAVING THE NEST

As soon as their young were old enough to leave their nests, the parents probably set off with the rest of the herd to another area where there was more rain and where green plants were lush.

Remains show that the young and old traveled together. Scientists have even found adult bones and the bones of young ones in three different sizes – perhaps one-, two-, and three-year-old Maiasaura. Once they had reached their new feeding grounds, the Maiasaura would spread out and spend their days browsing. Then, later in the year, they would return to the original nesting site to lay a new clutch of eggs and raise another family.

101

Muttaburrasaurus

Paleontologists believe that Muttaburrasaurus – just like Iguanodon – had a magnificent thumb spike on each hand and that this would have provided a deadly weapon, ideal for self-defense.

The sequence of illustrations *below* shows what might well have been an everyday event for a Muttaburrasaurus way back in Cretaceous times.

Imagine the scene. It is a warm, quiet afternoon in the depths of what is now Queensland, Australia. A young, lone Muttaburrasaurus has found an appetizing clump of weeds by some marshes and is chomping away, enjoying a tasty treat.

The young dinosaur, however, is too deeply engrossed in its meal to pay heed. So the flying reptiles now begin to squawk even more loudly, as if demanding attention.

Suddenly, a few flying reptiles begin squawking overhead, and they circle the Muttaburrasaurus as if in warning. The still of the region has been broken.

This time, the Muttaburrasaurus does look up and turns its head suspiciously. There could be predators around – dangerous flesh-eaters who would fight to the death if there was any chance at all of some delicious Muttaburrasaurus meat.

LIVED: Mid – Late Cretaceous times	**OTHER DATA:** Herbivore; mostly bipedal; thumb spikes; long tail; toothless beak; cheek teeth; nose bump
SIZE: 23ft (7m) long	
WEIGHT: 5 tons	
DISCOVERED: 1981, in Australia	**NAME MEANS:** "Muttaburra lizard"

ON THE SCENT

The Muttaburrasaurus sees nothing to worry it at first. Yet the flying reptiles are now making even louder noises. Muttaburrasaurus responds by sniffing at the air; and just as it catches the scent of meat-eaters, three mean-looking predators appear, leaping out from behind a group of tall trees where they have been lurking. They are Kakuru (KAK-<u>OO</u>-ROO) – much smaller than Muttaburrasaurus but very wily and extremely greedy carnivores nonetheless.

The nasty little beasts are just about to leap upon their victim as a pack when the larger dinosaur stabs at each of them in turn with both spikes. How the Kakuru howl in pain!

DINO FACT

When attacking an enemy with its thumb spikes, Muttaburrasaurus probably went for the neck or belly first.

As they snarl furiously in unison, it seems that Muttaburrasaurus will stand little chance. Its handy thumb spikes, however, will provide valuable protection. It has seen its parents use them against such enemies.

Speedily, they run off; but the wounds may be so great that, before too long, they will bleed to death. The Muttaburrasaurus has been saved by the warning given by the flying reptiles and by the strength of its own handy thumb spikes.

SUPERB SPECIMEN

Often, paleontologists have to make an educated guess as to how a dinosaur must have looked when it roamed Planet Earth all those millions of years ago. This is because only quite rarely is a whole skeleton unearthed. Such a "guess" will be based upon remains that have been found of similar species.

ON TWO LEGS OR FOUR

Muttaburrasaurus' back legs were quite strong, and it would have been able to rear up on them to reach for high-growing plants when feeding or to see for long distances. But it could also go along on all four limbs, which might have been easier.

Take a look now at the spiked thumbs on the front limbs of Muttaburrasaurus' skeleton. These spikes have not actually been found.

DINO FACT

Muttaburrasaurus was about the height of today's average adult man when it was resting on all-fours rather than standing erect.

Parrot-like beak

Nose bump

Powerful neck

With Muttaburrasaurus, however, they have been especially lucky. There is a particular skeleton that is the most complete of any dinosaur found in Australia so far, and this excellent specimen is on show at Brisbane's Queensland Museum.

As this drawing of its skeleton shows, Muttaburrasaurus was a strongly-built creature with a supple neck. Being able to move its neck easily helped it to feed and to spot predators.

Thumb spike

Long sturdy back limbs

104

However, Muttaburrasaurus is so similar to Iguanodon in other ways that scientists think that it, too, must have had the same type of inbuilt weapon. They have therefore reconstructed it with these.

NOSE BUMP

If you study Muttaburrasaurus' skull for a moment, you will spot that prominent bump over its nostrils. No one is quite sure what this was for. It may have helped to protect its head from attack; or perhaps, it has been suggested, the size of the bump helped males and females recognize each other – if, for instance, it was larger in the males.

Long tail

SHARP BEAK

You can also see from the skeleton that it had no teeth at the front of its mouth, which was beak-like – only in its cheeks. The beak was useful, of course, for stripping off vegetation, before Muttaburrasaurus cut up its meal with its battery of cheek teeth.

DAILY DIET

What, then, would Muttaburrasaurus have eaten by way of vegetation? Its diet probably comprised mainly horsetails and ferns, as well as leaves from tall trees, and maybe flowering plants that first appeared during Cretaceous times. (As yet, however, there was no grass to be found on Planet Earth.) The quantities it ate of all this vegetation were probably vast in the course of the day. In fact, it may hardly ever have stopped eating!

World of Muttaburrasaurus

- A site has been discovered near Winton in Queensland where a dinosaur stampede must have taken place over 100 million years ago.

- When trying to escape danger and running at top speed, Muttaburrasaurus probably did so on all-fours, rather than on its back legs only.

Ouranosaurus

First discovered in Africa's Sahara Desert in 1966, remains of Ouranosaurus show it was a very large creature with spiked thumbs, and a long sail-like structure all the way down its back and tail.

At first, scientists were puzzled about the purpose of that strange "sail" on Ouranosaurus' back. However, they have now come up with a very acceptable explanation.

It may somehow have been used as a heating and cooling system, to ensure that Ouranosaurus' body temperature was kept well-controlled and at an acceptable level.

Flat snout

Thumb spike

LIVED: Early Cretaceous times
SIZE: 23ft (7m) long
WEIGHT: 6.5 tons
DISCOVERED: 1966, in Africa

OTHER DATA: Quadrupedal/bipedal; sail structure along back and tail; herbivore; broad, flat snout; thumb spikes; cheek teeth
NAME MEANS: "Brave reptile"

Just as solar panels on some modern buildings take in heat from the sun, so blood in Ouranosaurus' sail could be warmed by the sun on a cool morning. Then, later in the day, Ouranosaurus could stand so that its "sail" did not absorb so much heat and it could cool down by releasing excess heat from this structure on its back.

DINO FACT

Ouranosaurus had leaf-shaped teeth and a strong bite, which were ideal for chomping up all the plant stuff that it ate.

Sail-like structure

Stiff tail

107

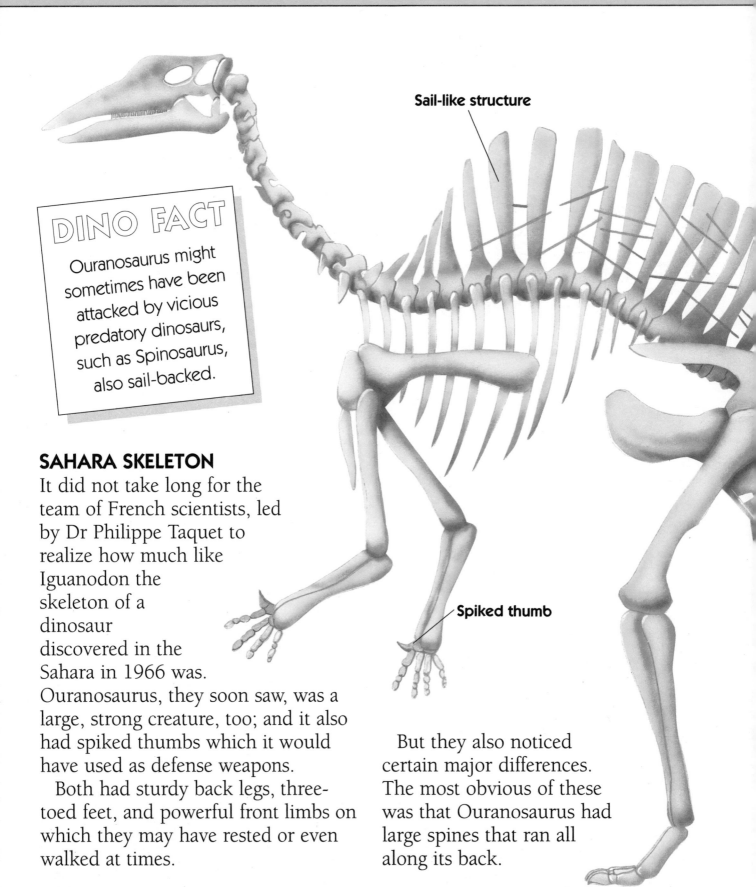

Sail-like structure

SAHARA SKELETON

It did not take long for the team of French scientists, led by Dr Philippe Taquet to realize how much like Iguanodon the skeleton of a dinosaur discovered in the Sahara in 1966 was. Ouranosaurus, they soon saw, was a large, strong creature, too; and it also had spiked thumbs which it would have used as defense weapons.

Both had sturdy back legs, three-toed feet, and powerful front limbs on which they may have rested or even walked at times.

Spiked thumb

But they also noticed certain major differences. The most obvious of these was that Ouranosaurus had large spines that ran all along its back.

108

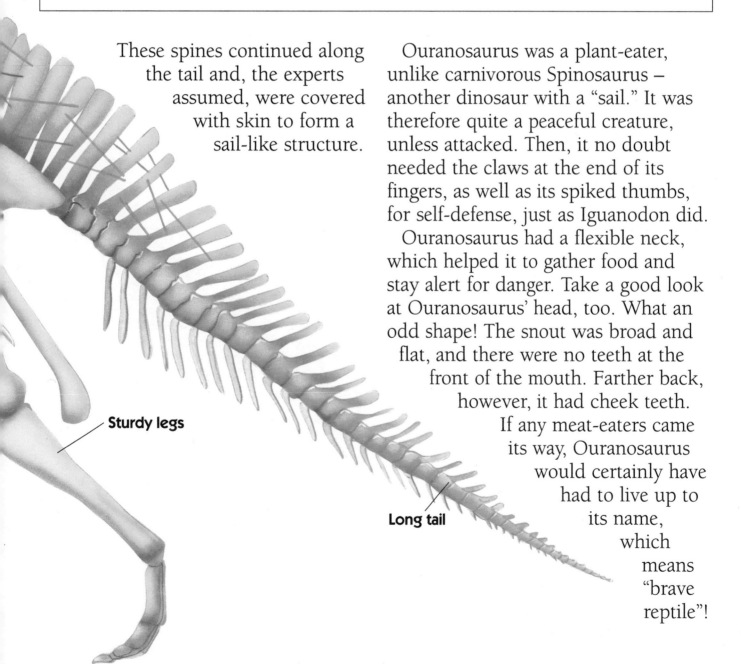

World of Ouranosaurus

- Lots of Ouranosaurus bones were found on the surface of the ground in the African country of Niger, where the wind, over great spans of time, had blown away layers of sand.

- Several African countries have what are known as "dinosaur beds," where many different types of dinosaur remains – and sometimes nests – have been found in large quantities.

These spines continued along the tail and, the experts assumed, were covered with skin to form a sail-like structure.

Ouranosaurus was a plant-eater, unlike carnivorous Spinosaurus – another dinosaur with a "sail." It was therefore quite a peaceful creature, unless attacked. Then, it no doubt needed the claws at the end of its fingers, as well as its spiked thumbs, for self-defense, just as Iguanodon did.

Ouranosaurus had a flexible neck, which helped it to gather food and stay alert for danger. Take a good look at Ouranosaurus' head, too. What an odd shape! The snout was broad and flat, and there were no teeth at the front of the mouth. Farther back, however, it had cheek teeth. If any meat-eaters came its way, Ouranosaurus would certainly have had to live up to its name, which means "brave reptile"!

Sturdy legs

Long tail

Oviraptor

Remains of Oviraptor were first found in Mongolia by a paleontologist named George Olsen in 1923, during an expedition organized by the American Museum of Natural History. Strangely, the skeleton indicated that there had been two prongs in the roof of its mouth instead of teeth.

A full-grown Oviraptor was probably about 6ft (2m) long, and only about as tall as an average 10-year-old boy. Looking very bird-like, it was quick on its feet and probably ran around on its two slim back legs, using clawed, three-fingered hands for grabbing.

Oviraptor had to be nimble because it needed to make a quick getaway at times, to escape predators and possibly to run off with stolen eggs on which paleontologists think it liked to feast.

CRACKING DINOSAUR

Eggs, fruit, nuts and snails would have been ideal foodstuffs for a dinosaur with no true teeth – just sharp prongs; and its horny beak would have been useful for cracking open a meal, too. Oviraptor's claws were also well adapted to holding something that was oval in shape and perhaps warm and slippery – like a new-laid egg.

When the remains of an Oviraptor were discovered for the first time, they were over a nest. Indeed, the condition of the skeleton seemed to suggest that the Oviraptor had been crushed to death by a furious Protoceratops parent as it tried to protect its eggs.

But scientists have recently come to change their viewpoint, saying that evidence found in Mongolia suggests Oviraptor had not actually been eating Protoceratops' eggs after all, but incubating its own.

Tarbosaurus

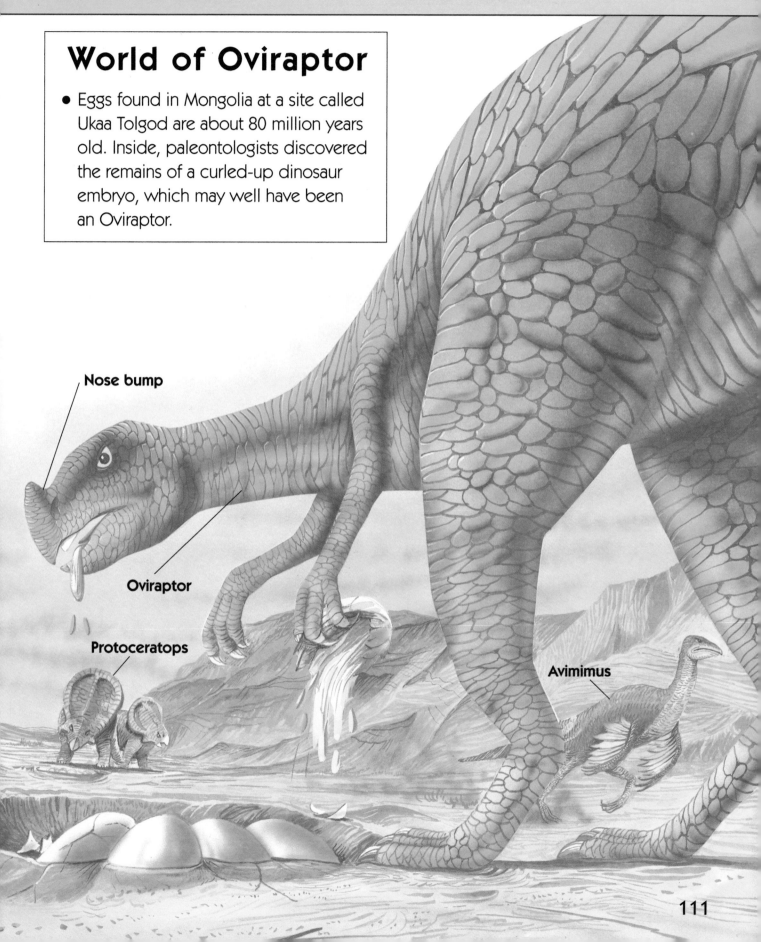

LIVED: Late Cretaceous times
SIZE: 6ft (2m) long
WEIGHT: 73lb (33kg)
DISCOVERED: 1923, in Mongolia

OTHER DATA: Speedy; two prongs instead of teeth; omnivore; crested head; liked eggs; unusual shoulder bones
NAME MEANS: "Egg thief"

World of Oviraptor

- Eggs found in Mongolia at a site called Ukaa Tolgod are about 80 million years old. Inside, paleontologists discovered the remains of a curled-up dinosaur embryo, which may well have been an Oviraptor.

Nose bump

Oviraptor

Protoceratops

Avimimus

111

UNUSUAL SKELETON

The first remains of Oviraptor to be dug up in Mongolia included just part

So the skulls that have been dug up are not all exactly like the one shown in this skeletal reconstruction.

Some had just a nose bump; but others, perhaps males, had more of a crest on their heads. Nevertheless, the heads all seem to have had strong but toothless jaws, covered in horn, and two strong prongs instead of teeth.

Toothless, two-pronged jaws

of the neck and a few ribs, as well as shoulder bones, a left forelimb and most of a right hand.

Since then, better skeletons have been discovered, however; and these show that Oviraptor was quite unusual for a dinosaur in two particular ways.

First of all, it had a collar bone in the shoulder that was shaped much like the wishbone that is pulled for good luck if a whole chicken has been cooked. Previously, scientists believed that no dinosaurs at all had a *single* bone in the shoulder like this. Instead, they thought dinosaurs always had a pair of shoulder bones. So leading paleontologists were quite surprised by this discovery.

They were astonished, too, when they realized that not all Oviraptor heads were quite the same.

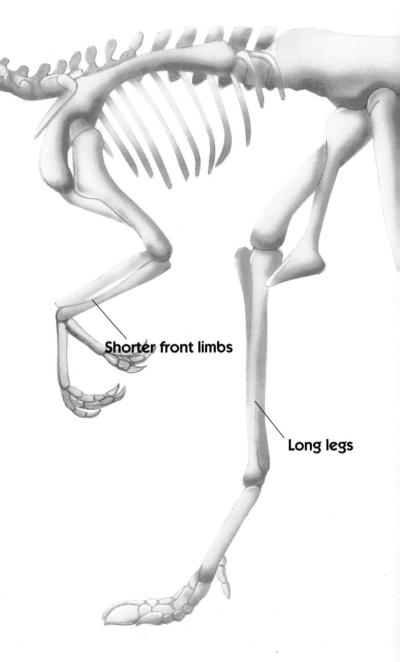

Shorter front limbs

Long legs

PIERCING BITE

The two prongs in Oviraptor's jaws were sharp and pointed downward for biting into the hard surfaces of large fruits, nuts and perhaps even snails, as well as eggs.

Its three clawed fingers on each hand were long and flexible, with the first finger a little shorter than the other two were.

It was used in much the same way as *we* use *our* thumbs today, to help us to grasp things.

Without this shorter finger, this egg-thief might never have managed to hold anything securely.

LEGS AND TAILS

Oviraptor's legs were quite slim and light – all the better for making a quick escape when needed. It was related to the ornithomimosaurs, ostrich-like dinosaurs that seem to have roamed Mongolia (though some have also been found in what is now western North

Stiff, tapering tail

America). All had long legs and lived in Cretaceous times.

Notice how Oviraptor's tail gradually tapered, getting thinner towards a point at the end. When it was standing still to feed, its tail may have drooped. But when Oviraptor ran, its tail was probably held out straight behind it, right off the ground at body level, to help it balance and gain speed.

And, finally, take a look at its three main toes that ended in sharp claws. Like many dinosaurs, Oviraptor also had an extra tiny, toe-like growth, as you can see.

DINO FACT

Other dinosaurs found in Mongolia include bird-like Gallimimus, frilled Protoceratops and beaked Psittacosaurus.

Pachycephalosaurus

Just look at this amazing beast! Its peculiar head looks rather like a crash helmet, with lots of bumpy pieces of bone for additional protection.

Pachycephalosaurus, measured about 15ft (4.6m) from the tip of its snout to the end of its tail. It would also have been more than twice the height of a fully grown human being of today when it reared up on its hind legs. But the most outstanding feature of this dinosaur was its domed skull. It was very thick on top and surrounded by lots of bony pieces.

LIVED:	Late Cretaceous times	OTHER DATA:	Herbivore; tough, high-domed skull;
SIZE:	15ft (4.6m) long		spiky snout; mostly bipedal; sturdy legs;
WEIGHT:	1 ton		smaller arms; five fingers; thick tail
DISCOVERED:	1940, in USA	NAME MEANS:	"Thick-headed lizard"

These bumps and spines gave Pachycephalosaurus the protection it needed for head-on fights. Its brain was not very large, but it still needed something to shield it from the impact and shock of head-to-head combat.

RIVAL MALES

Why, then, did this dinosaur get involved in fights? Pachycephalosaurus did not go out of its way to attack and kill other dinosaurs. It was a plant-eater and did not need to rely on other creatures for food. Instead, the males sparred with each other over mates and territory.

Pachycephalosaurus also used its skull as a battering ram if carnivorous dinosaurs attacked. Its thick skull therefore had to withstand an enormous amount of bashing.

Most skulls of Pachycephalosaurus have been found in low-lying areas. In fact, the very first specimen was found by paleontologist William Winkley in a valley in Montana, USA, in 1940. However, experts think they did not necessarily live in valleys but fairly high up, and in groups, out of the reach of such predators as T rex. So their skulls had probably been washed downstream to these lowlands.

BONE-HEAD'S SKELETON

Pachycephalosaurus, as you can see, stood on two back legs and had two shorter front limbs. But the most interesting part of its sturdy skeleton was its skull. About 10in (23cm) thick and 2ft (60cm) long, this must have been extremely impressive.

Helmet-like skull

Small rough-edged teeth

It is very rare for a paleontologist to find a whole dinosaur skull. This is because they were usually lightweight and broke up very easily over all the millions of years for which they lay buried under tons of rock. But it is fairly common for whole skulls of Pachycephalosaurus and its relatives to be unearthed during excavations for dinosaur remains because the bone was so thick.

HEADS DOWN

When the males head-butted a predator, or their rivals, in a battle of strength for a mate, they held their skulls downward, with their bodies horizontal to the ground. This meant that the force of the blows they struck could be absorbed by their thick necks, shoulders, and backbones. At the same time, the force of their head-butting would have had the full weight of their massive bodies behind it.

Five-fingered hands

Longer hind limbs

The impact of the skulls would have been very strong and loud as they crashed together over and over again during a contest.

World of Pachycephalosaurus

- All those head-banging matches required lots of energy, so – as an herbivore – Pachycephalosaurus probably ate huge quantities of vegetation several times a day.

- Some scientists think that a male Pachycephalosaurus may possibly have had a more brightly colored head than a female, to attract her when the mating season came round.

DINO POWER
Some of today's creatures that fight head-to-head (mountain sheep, for example) have spaces in their skulls.

Large eye sockets in the skull give us the clue that Pachycephalosaurus may have had sharp eyesight, helping it to spot any sign of danger.

Tapering tail

These are to dull the shock to the brain when they fight. Pachycephalosaurus, however, had no such spaces in its skull roof. Scientists think the creature's strong backbone absorbed much of the shock of head-butting. Otherwise, constantly using its head as a battering ram would have been exceedingly painful. Pachycephalosaurus held its long, tapering tail out stiffly behind as it ran, for better balance. Its hips, meanwhile, at the top of its back legs, were wide and helped strengthen its backbone.

BORN IN THE USA
Skeletons of Pachycephalosaurus have been found only in North America, while those of its relatives have been dug up elsewhere. The earliest-known bone-head was in fact dug up on the south coast of England. A 3ft (90cm)-long plant-eater, Yaverlandia (YAU-ERR-LAND-EE-A) was far smaller than its American relative, but also had two thick, bony areas capping its skull. Another possible relative's domed skull has also been found in Madagascar, an island situated off the southeast coast of Africa, in the Indian Ocean.

117

Parasaurolophus

A duck-billed, plant-eating dinosaur that roamed what is now North America, Parasaurolophus had a magnificent lengthy hollow tube rising from its head that was possibly larger in the males.

Most paleontologists now agree that Parasaurolophus – a giant herbivore from Cretaceous times – could bellow through its head crest, producing a long, low sound if it breathed out strongly through two of the four tubes that there were inside it.

HOLLOW THEORY

But this crest may well have had other functions, too. One theory originally put forward is that the hollow tube could perhaps have been used as a kind of snorkel under water.

Another possibility is that the crest could adjust itself to rest against the back of Parasaurolophus' neck. If so, this might have proved useful when Parasaurolophus was running through thick forest.

If this supposition was correct, the tubes in the crest could have provided tanks for storing air. However, this idea is actually now thought most unlikely.

An adjustable crest would not have become tangled in any overhanging vegetation.

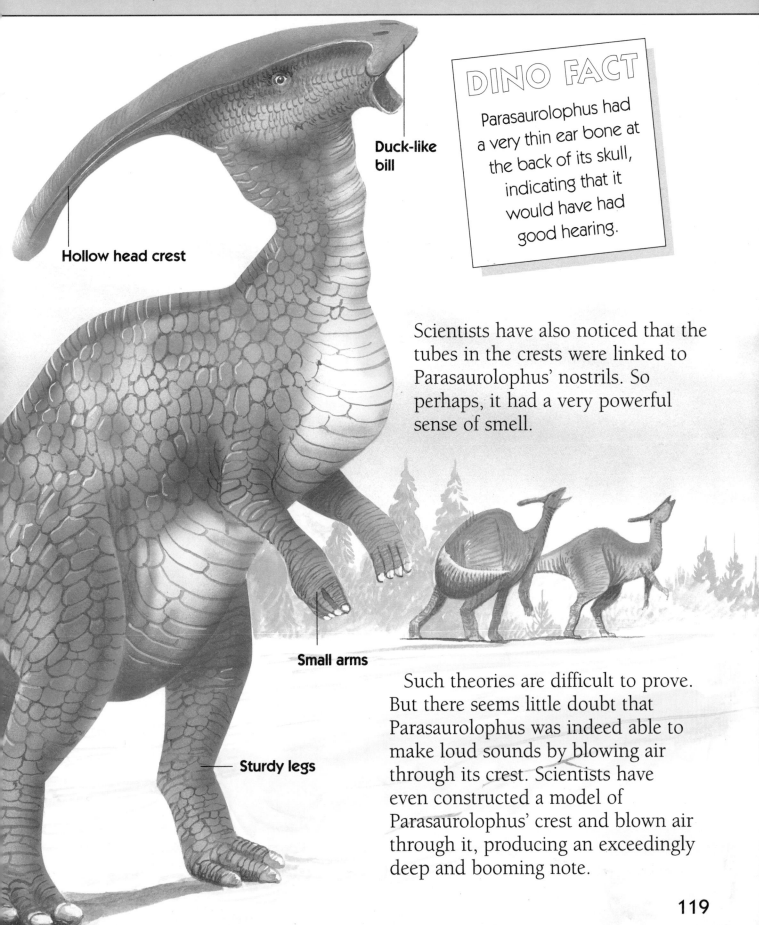

LIVED: Late Cretaceous times
SIZE: 33ft (10m) long
WEIGHT: 3 tons
DISCOVERED: 1922, in USA

OTHER DATA: Herbivore; mostly bipedal; huge hollow tube on head, through which it bellowed; duck-billed; cheek teeth
NAME MEANS: "Beside Saurolophus"

Duck-like bill

Hollow head crest

DINO FACT

Parasaurolophus had a very thin ear bone at the back of its skull, indicating that it would have had good hearing.

Scientists have also noticed that the tubes in the crests were linked to Parasaurolophus' nostrils. So perhaps, it had a very powerful sense of smell.

Small arms

Sturdy legs

Such theories are difficult to prove. But there seems little doubt that Parasaurolophus was indeed able to make loud sounds by blowing air through its crest. Scientists have even constructed a model of Parasaurolophus' crest and blown air through it, producing an exceedingly deep and booming note.

119

STRIKING SKELETON

Parasaurolophus was a heavily-built dinosaur with strong bones and joints. Its front limbs were practical in a number of ways. It could use them when walking, for example.

At the end of its shorter front limbs, Parasaurolophus had hands that were flat and shaped like paddles. Some scientists believe these could have been used to help it swim.

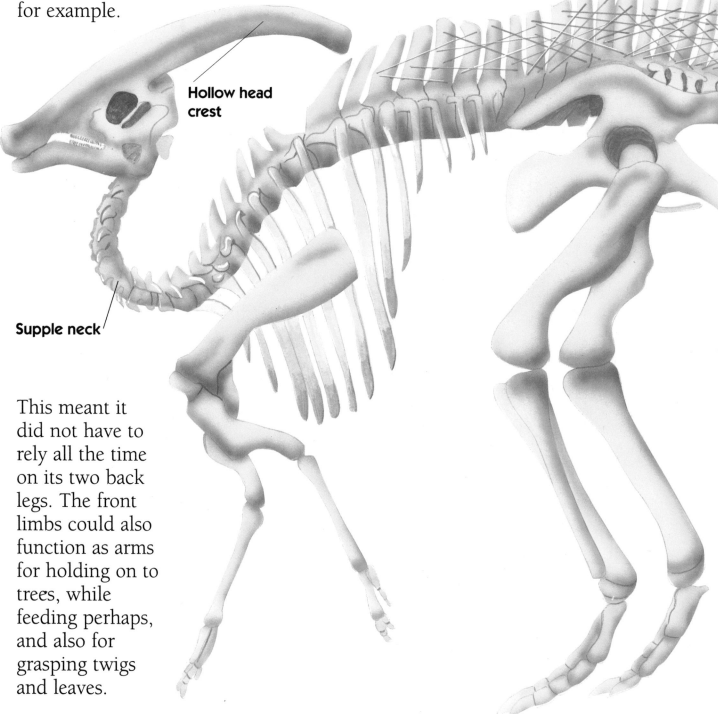

Hollow head crest

Supple neck

This meant it did not have to rely all the time on its two back legs. The front limbs could also function as arms for holding on to trees, while feeding perhaps, and also for grasping twigs and leaves.

However, on the whole, dinosaurs did not often take to the water.

Parasaurolophus weighed about three tons – as much as an adult elephant does today. So its ankle and toe bones had to be powerful enough to support all that weight.

Its teeth lined the upper and lower jaws towards the back of its mouth and formed a large surface which provided a sort of chopping board.

Like most other hadrosaurs, Parasaurolophus had a network of tough tendons among the bones that pointed up from its spine. These were especially strong around the dinosaur's hip bones. The long thin bones that pointed downward from its tail, meanwhile, gave it the strength to balance on its tail whenever it reared up to feed on tall trees.

Tapering tail

At the front of its mouth was a beak, used to snip off plants. It is usually described as a duck's bill but was strong and sharp – more like a turtle's beak, in fact. Parasaurolophus also had hundreds of small, diamond-shaped teeth.

Parasaurolophus probably had good control over its tail, which would have been something of an asset if ever it needed to use it as a weapon.

But the most spectacular feature of Parasaurolophus' body was, of course, that hollow head crest.

World of Parasaurolophus

- Relatives included Lambeosaurus (LAM-BEE-OH-SAW-RUS) which had a bulbous forward-pointing crest, and Coryosaurus (KO-REE-OH-SAW-RUS) with a thin head crest resembling a plate.

- Saurolophus (SAW-OH-LOAF-US), from which Parasaurolophus gets its name, also lived in Cretaceous North America, as well as Mongolia. Its head crest, however, had a far more modest spike.

121

Protoceratops

Protoceratops may have looked rather fierce. But it was small for a dinosaur and, like all herbivores, only ate plants and fought just in self-defense. From its skeletal remains, we can tell that it had a beaked mouth and a large, bony frill around the neck.

What is now Mongolia's Gobi Desert was once home to this squat, clumsy-looking dinosaur. Only about 6ft (1.8m) long and 3ft (90cm) tall when fully grown, Protoceratops had beaked jaws and a bizarre sort of frill extending from its neck, rather like a huge, round collar.

This would have been useful in times of danger, giving protection to its body, just like a shield.

Another tool for self-protection against predators was Protoceratops' large, thick tail which was almost as long as its body. It may have used the tail to whack at its enemies.

Neck frill

Longer back legs

Stubby toes

Lumpy protrusions

LIVED: Late Cretaceous times
SIZE: 6ft (1.8m) long
WEIGHT: 110lb (50kg)
DISCOVERED: 1923, in Mongolia

OTHER DATA: Herbivore; small; parrot-like beak; bony growths at side of face; bony neck frill; thick tail
NAME MEANS: "First-horned face"

LEADER OF THE PACK

At the start of the mating season, scientists think that a young male would challenge the old leader to see who would be head of the herd next. Standing a little way apart, they would roar at each other fiercely. Then they charged, butting each other with their bony heads. When at last the weaker one gave way, it was probably battered and bruised but not seriously hurt. It then took its place in the herd again, while the victor became the new leader of the pack.

HATCHING OUT

Herds of Protoceratops probably lived in peaceful groups, just like deer or elephants do today. Their numbers would have made it safer to rear their young – several Protoceratops together could fend off any predators. Many nests have been found that are very well preserved and contain fossilized eggs shaped like fat sausages rather than being round or oval. Tough shells would have protected the growing babies, curled up inside, from being crushed.

DINO FACT

Protoceratops had to guard its nest carefully against thieves, such as Oviraptor, which may have snatched a meal of eggs.

Thick tail

123

SMALL BUT POWERFUL

Protoceratops had a skeleton of strong, thick bone to hold up the weight of its bulky body, which was heavy for its small size. Scientists think that Protoceratops walked on all-fours. It could probably have run quite fast on its broad, strong, clawed feet when in danger for short periods, but it was usually content just to lumber along.

The skeletons of the males were probably much larger than those of the females.

Protoceratops skeletons also seem to have had differently shaped frills around their necks. Frills belonging to the males were probably bigger, too, just as their bodies were.

If you take a look at the size of Protoceratops' head, you will see that from the tip of its beak to the top of its frill, measured about half the length of its body, without the tail.

Protoceratops had a strange mouth.

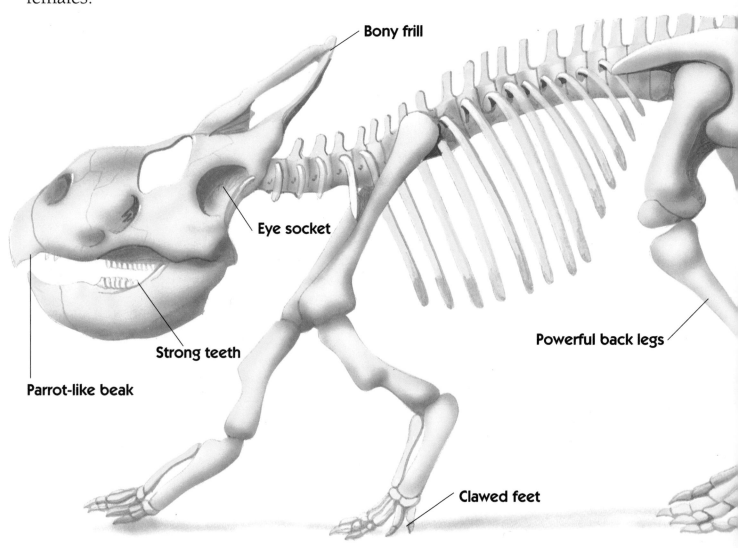

Bony frill

Eye socket

Strong teeth

Parrot-like beak

Powerful back legs

Clawed feet

World of Protoceratops

- Smaller Bagaceratops (BAG-AH-<u>SER</u>-A-TOPS) was a relative of Protoceratops and also lived in what is now Mongolia, as did Microceratops (MY-CROW-<u>SER</u>-A-TOPS), one of the tiniest dinosaurs ever found.

- Members of the Protoceratops family also included Montanaceratops (MON-TANA-<u>SER</u>-A-TOPS), found in Montana, USA. It, too, had a frill and also a prominent nose horn.

It was shaped like a curved beak. The top jaw was longer than the lower jaw, and there were no teeth at the front of the bony beak.

Thick, tapering tail

Instead, there were rows of teeth farther back in Protoceratops' mouth.

Protoceratops' jaws had strong muscles that helped it chew plants. It also had powerful muscles linked to the neck frill which were used for holding up its head.

The frill itself was like a round, flat collar, and was made of solid bone. It spread out backwards from its skull, and the bone had two large holes in it, to make it lighter.

Thousands of years ago, when the Chinese found bones and

teeth like those of this skeleton, they thought they belonged to dragons. But, of course, dragons never really existed. We now know that they were the bones of dinosaurs such as Protoceratops.

Psittacosaurus

The strangest thing about Psittacosaurus was its horny, toothless beak. This was rather like a parrot's, and was used for chopping off vegetation.

Psittacosaurus was not large by dinosaur standards – only around 3ft (1m) long, and weighing in at 35lb (15kg). It walked mainly on two back legs; but its forelimbs were not only useful for grabbing at the plants it ate, as a herbivore. In fact, it may also have walked on all-fours at times.

BABY FINDS

Many years after Psittacosaurus bones were first dug up in the 1920s, paleontologists noticed that among the remains there were a number of small skulls. These are thought to have come from Psittacosaurus babies.

Within the skulls, there were several worn teeth.

Parrot-like beak

LIVED: Early Cretaceous times
SIZE: 3ft (1m) long
WEIGHT: 35lb (15kg)
DISCOVERED: 1923, in Mongolia

OTHER DATA: Plant-eater; mostly bipedal; short arms; long legs; parrot-like beak; teeth at sides of mouth; swallowed gastroliths
NAME MEANS: 'Parrot lizard'

This seems to indicate that these particular babies were already feeding themselves.

If you could have looked inside an adult Psittacosaurus' mouth, you would have seen that it had no teeth at all behind its horny beak. Instead they were further back at the sides.

DINO FACT

Psittacosaurus was first described by Henry F. Osborn, the renowned American paleontologist, in 1923.

Like all the herbivorous dinosaurs, Psittacosaurus looked forward to meals of crisp leaves, fresh shoots and other nutritious plant food. The parrot-like beak from which its gets it name, meaning "parrot lizard," came in very handy for biting through tough vegetation, as in this illustration.

Powerful tail

127

World of Psittacosaurus

- Over one hundred gastroliths – stones and pebbles swallowed to help grind up food in a dinosaur's stomach and aid digestion of tough vegetable matter – have been found in the fossilized skeleton of a Psittacosaurus.

- Some scientists think it is possible that Psittacosaurus may have had a gizzard (a special part of the stomach that today's birds also have for breaking up hard food) to facilitate the processing and digestion of foodstuff.

In this description of a near encounter with a carnivore, we see how Psittacosaurus and another Cretaceous herbivore, Wuerhosaurus (WOO-ER-HOH-SAW-RUS) coped with such everyday dramas.

It was a stormy day in Early Cretaceous times, and groups of Psittacosaurus had taken shelter.

Now that the rain had almost stopped, however, they ventured out from under the huge trees to feed on low-lying plants and shrubs.

The thunder had died down and all was calm again. The only sounds now were occasional background snorts. These grunting noises came from the Psittacosaurus as they stopped to digest their meal from time to time.

The screeching of pterosaurs could be heard overhead, too.

It was just as well that the Psittacosaurus were small. This meant they did not have to compete with the Wuerhosaurus that were busy browsing in the same area. The Wuerhosaurus could reach up to higher branches for leaves.

They could sense the approach of a meat-eater and instinctively knew there was no time to lose.

A PREDATOR'S APPROACH

Quick as a flash, they began to scamper away, just as a dreadful roar and thudding footsteps started to resound through the valley.

These 20ft (6m)-long, four-legged plant-eaters had smaller heads than Psittacosaurus and two rows of plates along their backs. They had nasty tail spikes, too – useful whenever they needed to fight in self-defense against marauding predators. But they, too, spent most of their time just feeding on plants.

Then, all at once, both species of herbivores stopped what they were doing and sniffed the air.

Would these herbivores escape to survive another Cretaceous day? Or would one, or more, fall victim to a giant carnivore's terrible teeth and savage bite?

Life for plant-eaters 100 million years ago was generally peaceful. But they were always at risk from hungry carnivores that relished fresh dinosaur flesh, killing daily for meals.

129

Spinosaurus

What a strange sail-shaped appendage Spinosaurus sported on its back! Its purpose has certainly kept scientists guessing since Spinosaurus was first unearthed in Egypt in 1915. But experts now have an interesting theory to put forward about the part it may well have played in this dinosaur's daily life.

Sail with its back to the sun to cool down

Spinosaurus was many times taller than a human being is today. In fact, it was so enormous that it may even have eaten the equivalent of one hundred hamburgers every single day to satisfy its fantastic appetite! Spinosaurus was heavy, too. It may have weighed as much as sixty adult men!

In many respects, Spinosaurus was rather like most other large carnivores, with massive jaws just made for taking in great chunks of raw flesh. But there was one big difference. Spinosaurus also sported a huge sail-like structure on its back. This made it even larger and bulkier. At its central point, the sail alone was a lot taller than *you* are.

Another African dinosaur – Ouranosaurus – had a 'sail' quite like this, too, but somewhat smaller. This has led scientists to assume that such a sail might have had some special purpose – perhaps to help these dinosaurs survive in the type of climate that there was in that part of the world in Cretaceous times.

LIVED: Late Cretaceous times
SIZE: 50ft (15m) long
WEIGHT: 4 tons
DISCOVERED: 1915, in Egypt

OTHER DATA: Carnivore; bipedal; large sail on back; bulky body; huge straight teeth; crocodile-like jaws; thick tail
NAME MEANS: "Spine lizard"

AIR CONDITIONING

In the middle of the day, for instance, Spinosaurus might have stood with its back to the sun, as you can see in the picture on the facing page. This would have prevented the sail from absorbing the sun's warmth so that Spinosaurus, which may have been cold-blooded, did not overheat. If, by chance, the beast did get too hot, maybe it could also have taken a dip in a nearby lake or river and submerged its sail a few times in the water to help it cool down until the sun set.

SOLAR HEATING

But in the early morning, even in warm Cretaceous times, temperatures were probably not as high as later on in the day. It may even occasionally have been a bit chilly for Spinosaurus at dawn. So perhaps then, Spinosaurus stood so that its sail faced the sun and absorbed what warmth it could, as shown in the illustration *below*.

An alternative theory, however, is that sails of this kind may have been some form of sexual display to attract females during the mating season.

Sail side-on to the sun for warmth

SPINED SKELETON

About 50ft (15m) long from the end of its jaws to the tip of its tail – that's more than the length of a bus – Spinosaurus must have been one of the most feared creatures of Late Cretaceous times.

The tallest spines were central; and the spines themselves were narrower in the middle than at the top end.

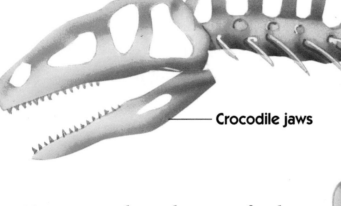

Crocodile jaws

You can see here the row of tail spines – the largest measuring about 6ft (1.8m) in height – that supported Spinosaurus' sail.

Clawed hands

World of Spinosaurus

- Spinosaurus was given its name – meaning "spine lizard" – by the eminent German paleontologist W. Ernst Stromer von Rechenbach who first discovered the remains of this dinosaur in Egypt, northern Africa, in 1915.

- Unfortunately, the first Spinosaurus remains to have been unearthed were destroyed during World War II in a bombing raid. But, luckily, other Spinosaurus bones have since been discovered in Niger, also in Africa.

High spines, forming a sail

When originally covered with skin, this structure must indeed have looked much like a sail.

HANDY FOOT CLAWS

Two strong, pillar-like legs supported Spinosaurus' weight, and its feet ended in three sharp claws. There was also an additional smaller, weak toe. Spinosaurus' larger foot claws must have come in useful for holding down victims as they tried to escape.

Spinosaurus' forelimbs were short but very powerful, too.

DINO FACT

One of Spinosaurus' most likely victims was huge Aegyptosaurus (AY-JIPT-OH-<u>SAW</u>-RUS), a North African herbivore, possibly 52ft (16m) high.

Powerful tail

Pillar-like legs

STRAIGHT TEETH

Spinosaurus' skull was very much like that of other large carnivorous dinosaurs, but the teeth were straighter. However, they were still as sharp as steak knives, and could easily have bitten through even the very toughest skin of any prey.

Spinosaurus' tail was long, broad and powerful. It might even at times, experts suggest, have been used to knock out an unfortunate victim with a series of dreadful blows.

Triceratops

Triceratops did not have to run from danger. It could easily fight off an attacker, probably in the same way that a rhino does today, by putting its head down and charging the enemy. With its powerful horns, Triceratops was a match for even the biggest carnivores.

It was because of its huge horns – one above each of its eyes and one smaller one on its nose – that Triceratops was given a name meaning "three-horned face." These horns were sharp and made nasty weapons that were useful for driving off predators like T rex. In fact, some scientists think that there may have been two or three different types of Triceratops since some skeletons seem to have had different kinds of horn.

Triceratops' head was enormous, as you can see in this depiction of three of these dinosaurs charging.

What was more, its head was crowned by a stiff, upright frill of bone. This was another of Triceratops' defense weapons.

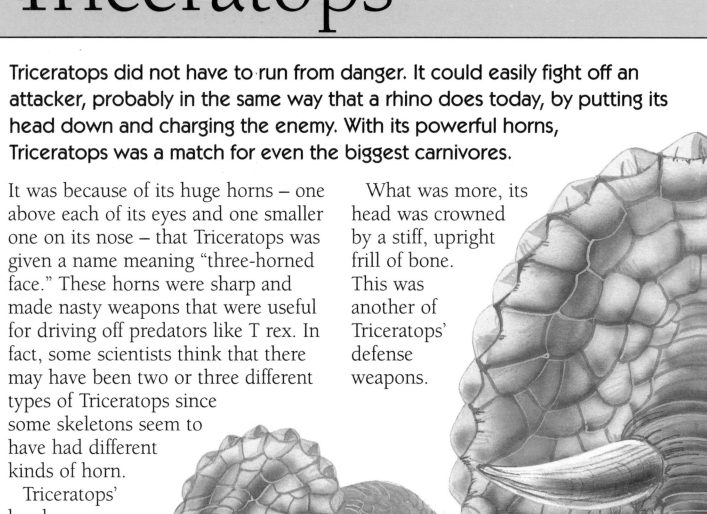

Nose horn

LIVED: Late Cretacous times
SIZE: 30ft (9m) long
WEIGHT: 6 tons
DISCOVERED: 1887, in USA

OTHER DATA: Herbivore; large neck frill; nose horn; two brow horns; beak; cheek teeth; hooved feet; long, thick tail
NAME MEANS: "Three-horned face"

The frill was also possibly used to show off when attracting a mate.

HUNDREDS OF TEETH

Triceratops was an herbivore, as scientists know from its teeth. It had hundreds of them all along the sides of its mouth, which wore out from time to time.

Eyebrow horns

But if this happened, from all that chomping on vegetation, new ones grew in their place. At the front of its face, meanwhile, Triceratops had a large curved beak with which it could bite off tough leaves and stalks.

THICK-SKINNED

Most dinosaurs had scaly skin. But Triceratops seems to have had an especially thick body covering. The scales possibly even formed a pattern, looking rather like a mosaic of tiles. Triceratops also had points on its cheeks, and thick knobs covered its body. Notice, too, the jagged bony edges of its frill.

Bony edge to neck frill

Sturdy feet

135

HEAD WRESTLERS

Triceratops' horns were mainly useful for driving off predators, but they had other uses as well. It is not difficult to guess what some of these uses may have been.

DINO FACT

Triceratops could probably run ten times as fast as you can when charging each other. Just imagine what the impact was like!

The male who wins the most matches then drives the other males away. He is now left to be leader of the herd – until he is challenged again for the leadership.

Triceratops may have lived in herds because so many bones have been found and dug up together in one place. So millions of years ago, Triceratops males may also have fought over leadership of the herd.

Brow horn

Thick, muscular tail

Nose horn

Consider how some of today's creatures use body weapons of this kind. Deer, for example, have antlers on their heads, and males use these to fight each other, clashing them together in a kind of wrestling match.

They may also have fought over mates, just like the deer of today.

Scientists have even found marks on Triceratops' neck frills, showing where they had become damaged during the course of such fights.

World of Triceratops

- On the bottom of each back foot, Triceratops had a special pad that provided a cushioned sole to protect it from rough ground and to help it walk more comfortably.

- Having found marks on the bone of Triceratops' neck frill, scientists know it was once covered with muscles that would have helped to move its jaws as it ate its meals of plant stuff.

Bony frill

Bumpy skin

Hooved feet

The sight of two enormous male Triceratops crashing into each other and doing battle must have been truly amazing.

PROTECTING THE YOUNG

If, as must sometimes have happened, a predator threatened to attack a mother Triceratops' young, the rest of the herd may well have formed an outward-facing ring to protect it.

Troodon

Seventy-five million years ago, on moonlit nights or by day, packs of Troodon, hungry for a meal of flesh, no doubt often stalked unwary victims and then suddenly took them by surprise.

Take a trip back in time and imagine a night when a full moon shone brightly, lighting up the edge of a Cretaceous forest, deep in the heart of what is now Canada.

Silently, they lurked by some thick bushes, keeping a constant eye out for unsuspecting prey. Troodon was a small dinosaur. But, more often than not, it was a very successful predator.

Whenever clouds passed over the moon, the forest would darken. But this was not a problem for a Troodon.

Here, the climate was much warmer then than it is today; even the nights were fairly warm, too.

On just such a night, a pack of Troodon – four in number – hungered for a meal of freshly-caught flesh.

Its eyesight was excellent, even in poor light; and with all its senses alert, it was bound to spot a likely victim before too long.

LIVED: Late Cretaceous times
SIZE: 6ft (2m) long
WEIGHT: 110lb (50kg)
DISCOVERED: 1856, in Canada

OTHER DATA: Bipedal; carnivore; speedy; sickle-shaped claw on foot; stiff tail; highly intelligent; long jaws; sharp teeth
NAME MEANS: "Wounding tooth"

What was that? Suddenly, a rustling could be heard among the bushes. Another type of carnivore was also on the prowl. It, too, was a speedy and awesome predator. But what chance did it stand against a whole pack of intelligent Troodon?

Quick as a flash, the pack of four dinosaurs encircled their victim and began to attack with their sickle claws. But the lone carnivore had claws like these, too, and so a vicious battle began, terrifying shrieks breaking the silence of the night.

The lone carnivore now sank to the ground, its heart beating rapidly. Death then came quickly. Its raw meat would provide an appetizing meal for the pack of famished Troodon, but they would soon be hungry again. Clearly, there were great advantages to hunting in packs in this way.

DINO FACT

Troodon had large and partly forward-facing eyes, probably helping it to judge distance particularly accurately – a help when hunting.

But eight sickle claws dealt eight dreadful wounds. It was all too much for the lone hunter. The pack of Troodon had overcome their victim.

SLIM AND SWIFT

Paleontologists have not been lucky enough to find a complete skeleton of Troodon. To date, they have only unearthed a few of its bones. Still, they have been able to compare these with remains of similar dinosaurs and have come up with a fairly good picture.

In fact, it was only about *your* height when it was running with its head almost level with the rest of its body.

SAW-LIKE TEETH

Troodon's jaws, we know, were lined with lots of short, saw-edged teeth, and there were many more than in most theropods. Such teeth would have been well suited to holding on to slippery prey – even fish, perhaps – and to ripping and slicing into flesh.

But lightweight as it was, Troodon was still a killer carnivore.

Long, slim jaws

Three-fingered hands

Long, slim legs

This skeletal reconstruction shows what Troodon must have looked like when on the move.

Surprisingly, though, Troodon – in spite of being a successful hunter – was not large in size – only some 6ft (2m) long.

DINO FACT

It is because of its small but sharp and partly-serrated teeth that Troodon was given its name, meaning "wounding tooth."

Sickle claw

World of Troodon

- Some experts have joked that if Troodon had not become extinct, it might eventually have developed an upright posture and become somewhat human-like in appearance.

- Intelligent Troodon is known to have had a very big brain for its body size. Experts can tell this from fossilized brain casing that has been found in Dinosaur Provincial Park, Canada.

GRAB THAT!

Troodon had fairly long arms, ending in three sharply-clawed fingers that were highly flexible. These would have

Bony rods held Troodon's tail straight out behind it, stiffly in position, as this sharp-witted, little hunter ran through the Cretaceous landscape.

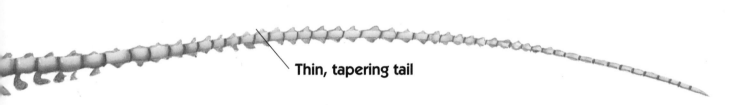

Thin, tapering tail

been ideal for grasping any wriggling creature trying to escape its clutches.

But it was the large retractable claw on one toe of each foot that provided an ideal weapon for actually stabbing a victim as it struggled to get free from Troodon's hold. Special muscles made it easy for these claws to be moved up and down whenever Troodon needed to slash out at its prey, thereby causing a nasty wound and no doubt great pain, too.

SUPER-INTELLIGENT

Many paleontologists think that Troodon's well-developed forebrain would have provided excellent hand-eye coordination, a useful skill when hunting. Theropods were, in general, the most intelligent dinosaurs of all. In fact, they probably needed to be because they had to rely upon their wits for catching a victim that would provide each meal. And it was coelurosaurs, such as Troodon, who seem to have been the brainiest of all.

Tyrannosaurus rex

One of the fiercest carnivores ever to have lived on Planet Earth, Tyrannosaurus rex was so huge that *you* would hardly have reached up to its knees. What an awesome monster it was!

Tyrannosurus rex, seen here confronting a Triceratops, had such enormous jaws that it could easily have swallowed whole many creatures of its time.

The first fairly good skeleton of a T rex was dug up in 1902, in Montana, USA, and soon identifed by the famous fossil-hunter Henry Fairfield Osborn, who gave this dinosaur its name.

Thick tail

Massive back legs

LIVED: Late Cretaceous times
SIZE: 39ft (12m) long
WEIGHT: 7 tons
DISCOVERED: 1902, in USA

OTHER DATA: Bipedal; carnivore; tiny arms; large jaws; two-fingered hands; sharp, serrated teeth
NAME MEANS: "King of the tyrant reptiles"

The first remains included parts of the skull and jaws, shoulder, hips and legs. From these alone, Osborn could tell it was enormous.

Tyrannosaurus rex was certainly huge and exceedingly heavy. In fact, its massive back legs had to support a tremendous amount of weight, possibly as much as 7 tons in all.

Huge jaws

Tiny arms

Windows in lightweight skull

Its hands were too far from T rex's mouth to be used for feeding. So experts have reached the conclusion that it must have used its great jaws to eat directly from a carcass. Its neck was thick and muscular, which meant it could twist and turn its head when tearing at its prey; and its skull was very large and strong but lightweight.

BIG BONES

From skeletal remains that have been unearthed, we know that T rex's back feet were very large and would have been around six times as long as *yours*. Each back foot had four toes, three facing forward and with extremely sharp, curved claws where we have toenails. Its toe bones were locked together for additional strength. The fourth toe faced backward and did not even touch the ground.

In comparison, T rex's front limbs were tiny and had at their extremities just two clawed fingers.

Two-fingered hands

DINO FACT

T rex is most likely to have lived alone or in a small family group, not in herds. It ate its own weight in meat every few days.

Long, strong legs

With its powerful jaw muscles, it could take giant bites of meat and crunch up bones with its enormous serrated fangs. If a tooth broke off as it ate, another probably grew in its place.

UPRIGHT STANCE

When T rex walked, it would hold its stiff tail level with its back to help it balance, and had its head raised, just as in this illustration of its skeleton.

T rex was so tall that it could easily have looked into an upstairs bedroom window of a two-story house, and was the length of several family-sized cars.

Long, stiff tail

Although it was so colossal, T rex may have been able to run remarkably fast over short distances, holding its stiff tail erect as an aid to balancing. Experts gather this from its long ankle bones. A predatory T rex must actually have been one of the most horrifying sights on Earth in prehistoric times.

Tyrannosaurus rex was actually one of the very last North American dinosaurs, and it would have been there at the time of their extinction, however this came about. It had no real competition from other dinosaurs, and could produce, with its jaws, a wound that would have been 3ft (1m) long. Hell Creek, in which some of its remains have been found, seems to be aptly named.

World of Tyrannosaurus

- Remains of T rex have been found not only in North America but in China, too.

- Scientists think that T rex probably let out a most terrifying roar as it was about to attack, and that this would have reverberated for a long way.

- Among those dinosaurs that might have fallen victim to a predatory T rex that was eager for a kill were Parasaurolophus, Troodon, Pachycephalosaurus and Maiasaura – all from what is now North America.

Velociraptor

Built for speed – as its long, slim limbs clearly show – Velociraptor was nowhere near as big as T rex, but it was still one of the most greatly feared predators of the age of the dinosaurs.

Scientists believe that Velociraptor may have hunted for food either alone or in small packs. Once a potential victim had been spotted, Velociraptor would race up to it, giving chase if it tried to run off. However, if it stood its ground and tried to put up some attempt at defence, Velociraptor would prance around, keeping just out of the range of the victim's butting head and lashing tail at first, until the carnivore grew weary of this sparring match and decided to make a move.

IN FOR THE KILL

At this point, Velociraptor would go in for the kill. Lunging forward, it would try to grab its victim's neck or head with its grasping fingers and vicious jaws. Once it had a good grip, the victim could not pull away from Velociraptor, however hard it tried.

Now that Velociraptor had sunk its teeth and claws into its prey – possibly a dinosaur like the young Homacephale (HOM-A-SEF-AL-EE) shown in this illustration – the injuries inflicted were almost bound to be fatal.

Next, standing on one leg and balancing with the help of its long, stiff tail, it would slash cruelly at the victim's soft underside with the large, curved, retractable claw on its second toe, tearing at the victim's leathery skin.

Its belly was probably soft and easily ripped open by that nasty claw.

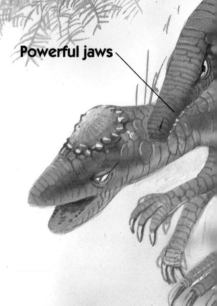

Powerful jaws

World of Velociraptor

- Velociraptor remains found in the Gobi Desert of Mongolia show that it died clutching a Protoceratops' skull.

- Velociraptor belonged to a family known as the Dromaeosaurids (DROM-EYE-OH-SAW-RIDS). All were speedy hunters.

LIVED: Late Cretaceous times
SIZE: 6ft (1.8m) long
WEIGHT: 33lb (15kg)
DISCOVERED: 1924, Mongolia

OTHER DATA: Carnivore; very speedy; powerful jaws; slashing claw on second toe of each foot; long, stiff tail; sharp teeth; big brain
NAME MEANS: "Quick plunderer"

Long, stiff tail

Retractable claw on second toe

147

FIERCE HUNTER

Velociraptor was a small, strong, speedy, carnivorous dinosaur, always on the look-out for a meal. But which of its body parts in particular helped make it such a ferocious hunter?

First of all, on its long, powerful arms, it had three very strong fingers, ending in sharp, long claws, as you can see *above*. When it got close enough, Velociraptor would grab its prey with these powerful hand claws, digging them in and holding on tightly for all it was worth. There would be no escape.

Most dinosaurs had three forward-pointing toes, each about the same length. Velociraptor, however, had four clawed toes on each foot.

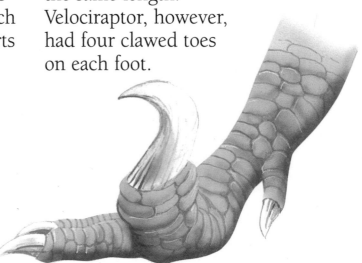

Yet it walked and ran on the third and fourth toes only. It was the second toe that bore Velociraptor's special claw, shown *above*. The first toe, meanwhile, was much smaller, pointed backward, and was of little use.

DINO FACT

Wonderful robotic models of terrifying Velociraptor feature in Steven Spielberg's blockbuster movie *Jurassic Park*.

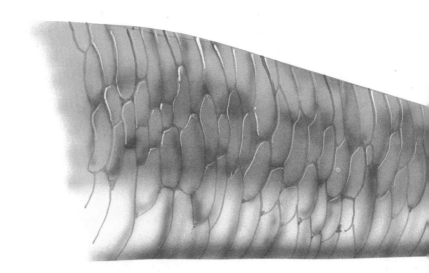

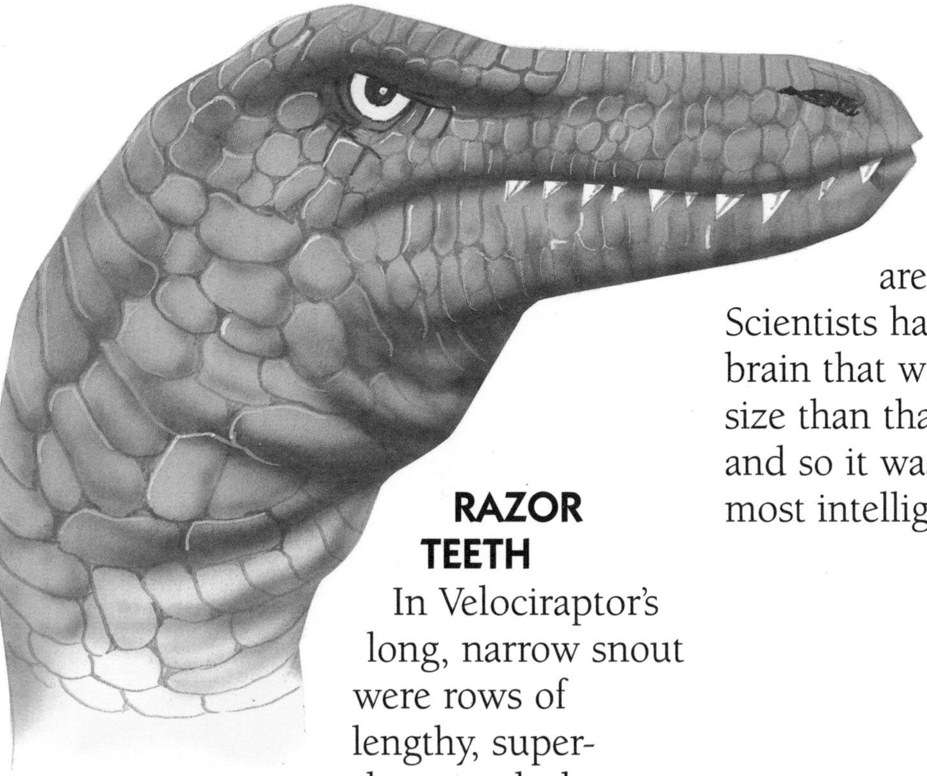

BIG BRAIN

Velociraptor, as you can see *below*, had large sockets for its eyes, which means the chances are it had very good sight. Scientists have also found that it had a brain that was much larger for its body size than that of most other dinosaurs, and so it was probably among the most intelligent and wily.

RAZOR TEETH

In Velociraptor's long, narrow snout were rows of lengthy, super-sharp teeth that curved slightly backward – ideal for coping with prey. The top set even possibly overlapped the bottom ones, giving it an extremely strong bite.

USEFUL TAIL

Velociraptor's tail was stiffened by bony rods. It would have been of little use as a weapon, however, but helped Velociraptor keep its balance at top speed while it was chasing its victims.

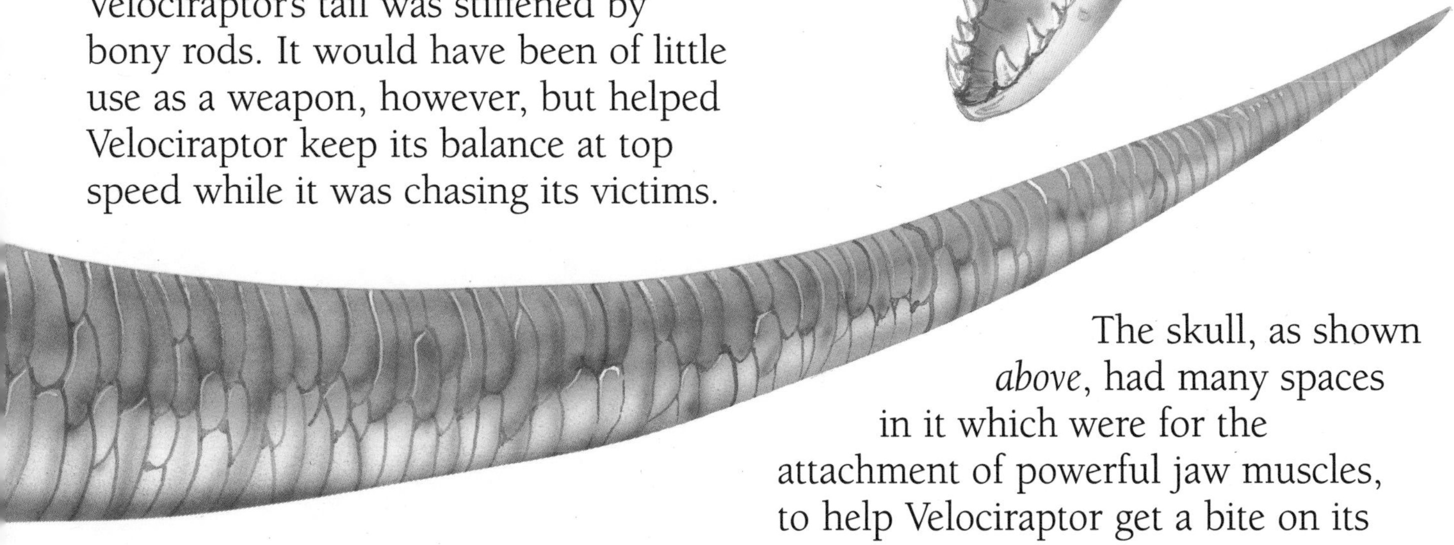

The skull, as shown *above*, had many spaces in it which were for the attachment of powerful jaw muscles, to help Velociraptor get a bite on its struggling prey.

149

Discovering

When young Henry Fairfield Osborn pretended to go dinosaur-hunting, little did he know that, as an adult, he would go on to make some world-famous discoveries of entirely new dinosaurs.

Back in 1876, Henry Fairfield Osborn laughed and joked with a friend one hot summer's day as they dried off after a cooling swim. As they chatted, the idea suddenly occurred to the boys that they should play at imaginary dinosaur-hunting.

ON SAFARI

Osborn thought this would be fun even if they failed to find any, and so the boys began a fantasy dinosaur safari.

Not unexpectedly, dinosaurs being long extinct, the game proved entirely unfruitful. Somehow, though, it must have left the seed of an ambition with Osborn, for that fantasy safari proved to be the starting point for a later career in paleontology in which he was to make his mark.

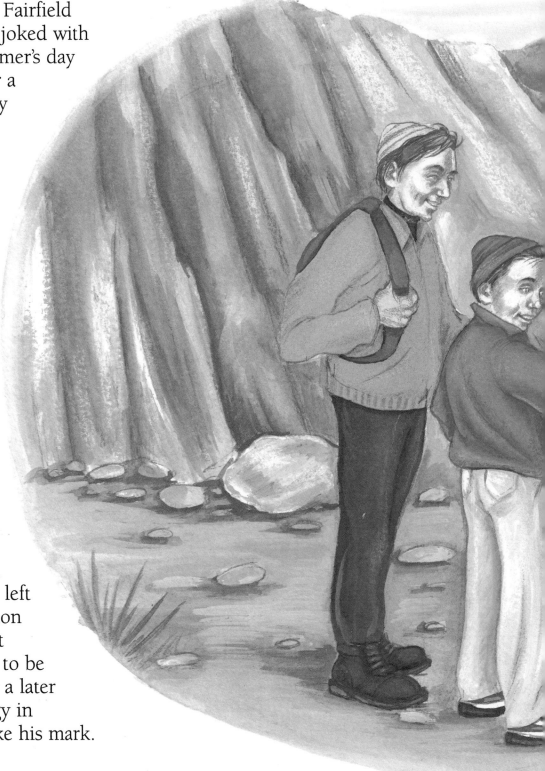

dinosaurs

Indeed, Henry Fairfield Osborn was eventually to become one of the world's greatest names in the study of prehistoric creatures.

Among Osborn's major projects were explorations at the Como Bluff and Bone Cabin quarries in the American state of Wyoming. Here, his team of workers unearthed countless dinosaur fossils; and in a period of six years, succeeded in digging up as much as 75 tons of dinosaur bones in all.

BONE PROPS

In fact, there were so many dinosaur bones scattered around this region that a certain farmer, not realizing what they were, had been using some as beams and props to build a cabin – which is how Bone Cabin Quarry got its name. And it was in this very quarry that the fossilized remains of Ornitholestes were discovered first.

On the pages that follow within this section, we present many other famous dinosaur discoveries made by amateurs and professionals alike. Maybe, some day you, too, might find some dinosaur fossils quite by chance, just like the family out walking in this picture!

It may seem hard to believe but, in 19th century America, rivalry over dinosaur finds was taken to such extremes that fighting actually broke out on occasions between teams of fossil-hunters.

In 1870, Edward Drinker Cope proudly showed Professor Othniel Charles Marsh, another respected paleontologist, the skeleton of a plesiosaur that he had been studying. Marsh was not at all impressed, however, pointing out that Cope had made a terrible mistake.

HEADS OR TAILS?

In reconstructing this sea creature that dated from the time of the dinosaurs, he had placed the head at the wrong end of the skeleton!

Key facts

- Between them, Marsh and Cope were responsible for discovering well over one hundred different dinosaurs.

- Many of the finds made during the Bone Wars are now in such major collections as the Smithsonian Institution, Washington D.C., the Peabody Museum at Yale and the American Museum of Natural History in New York.

Wars

Cope felt utterly embarrassed at his error, and the event was to herald many years of bitter rivalry between the two Americans.

FOSSIL FEUD

Both men continually strove to be the first to lay claim to new dinosaur discoveries in Colorado, Wyoming, Montana and New Mexico. Indeed, brawls sometimes broke out between the men working for each of them over interesting specimens. These became known as the "Bone Wars." But there was in fact a good side to all this, if only because such competition drove both men on to find more and more remains including those of such dinosaurs as Apatosaurus, Coelophysis, Triceratops and Allosaurus.

PRIZE EXHIBITS

Meanwhile, dinosaurs were all the rage and businessmen were becoming keen on sponsoring digs. Andrew Carnegie, in particular, was anxious to get hold of a really big dinosaur for his new museum in Pittsburgh, USA, and managed to acquire a huge Diplodocus skeleton. This became so greatly admired that King Edward VII of England asked for a life-size replica to be made. It took two years to construct and still holds pride of place at London's Natural History Museum.

As has often proved the case, dinosaur fossils sometimes turn up in quite unexpected places, and have to be identified speedily or they may be stolen or even lost forever.

One afternoon, a rancher working in Muttaburra, an area of central Queensland, Australia, contacted the Queensland Museum in great excitement. On the banks of the Thomson River, where his cattle had been grazing, he was amazed to find what looked like the remains of a dinosaur!

FOSSIL SOUVENIRS
The cattle had obviously been curious about the exposed bones and had scattered them about. Worse still, people living nearby, who had also recognized what the fossils were, had quite openly taken some of them as souvenirs.

At first, the museum doubted what the rancher claimed to have come across, but he was adamant. They therefore agreed to investigate and found he had been right.

PIECING IT TOGETHER

The local population later returned what they had taken.

It is just as well that they did, or experts might never have been able to piece together the remains of a most remarkable prehistoric creature, the first of this species of dinosaur to be found. Scientists later named the unique specimen Muttaburrasaurus langdoni, after the place where it had been found and also the rancher who had first reported it, and whose name was Langdon.

The reconstructed Cretaceous remains of Muttaburrasaurus – which is a member of the same family as Iguanodon with a bulging muzzle and large thumb claws – can now be seen in the Queensland Museum.

The great Gobi

Not until paleontologists found the remains of Protoceratops' nests and a considerable number of eggs in the Gobi Desert did they have confirmation for the first time that dinosaurs were not mammals after all.

Back in the 1920s, a group of scientists from the American Museum of Natural History went on an expedition to the Gobi Desert of Mongolia. They were hoping to find proof that the first human beings had lived there and to learn something about them.

After many months of exploration, the scientists found nothing by way of evidence concerning early humans. Then, suddenly, they made a very exciting discovery. In an area called Flaming Cliffs, because of the red color of its rocks, the explorers came across many fossilized dinosaur nests, filled with eggs. What was more, near to the nests, there were also lots of bones that seemed to come from a strange dinosaur with a frill around its neck.

egg finds

NESTING SITE

Close by, too, they found the fossilized bones of tiny, newly-hatched dinosaurs, a few unborn babies, and hundreds of pieces of shell. The scientists had stumbled across something very special – the first dinosaur eggs ever to be found, belonging to two new dinosaurs that were later named Protoceratops and Oviraptor.

Key facts

- Some nests were round, like shallow basins, and dug into sand.

- Dinosaur nests were often built in groups or colonies.

From these finds, scientists were able to tell that when a nest was ready, a mother would carefully drop each egg to form a neat spiral arrangement within it.

It is exciting enough when any new dinosaur find is made. But a discovery that dates all the way back to Triassic times – when these creatures first evolved – is all the more remarkable in that it was made by an amateur.

David Baldwin was not a professional paleontologist, working only as an occasional helper on l9th-century American digs. Yet it was he who made one of the most fascinating discoveries of his time.

Sometimes, Baldwin had assisted the well-known paleontologist Othniel C. Marsh, but later turned to helping Marsh's great rival, Edward D. Cope. However, he refused to work as part of any team, far preferring to dig independently and then send back any finds for expert identification.

EARLY REMAINS

So it was that, having unearthed some rather scrappy remains in Triassic rocks at a site near Abiquiu in New Mexico, Baldwin decided to send his finds on to Cope. The fossilized pieces of bone were immediately recognized as having belonged to a small, lightly-built carnivore – Coelophysis, one of the very first dinosaurs to evolve.

Ghost Ranch

EXPERT'S ERROR

The bones – bits of leg, vertebrae, pelvis and ribs – did not make up a complete skeleton, however; and so Cope assumed that they belonged to three different types of Coelophysis.

Later, though, he was to be proved wrong. In the world of paleontology, as in other fields, even the experts sometimes make an error! Cope had mistaken what were actually three different ages and sizes of Coelophysis for three different species of this particular dinosaur.

FURTHER FINDS

Many years later, an expedition returned to the New Mexico site, which by then had become part of an estate called Ghost Ranch. The trip proved worthwhile, for they did indeed find many further remains of this Triassic dinosaur. In fact, when they excavated a hillside, they unearthed dozens of skeletons in all. These were the remains of several dinosaurs – adults and young – that had probably perished in some sort of flash flood.

Key facts

- David Baldwin was the first to discover Coelophysis bones in New Mexico in 1881.

- Almost one hundred skeletons of Coelophysis were finally dug up at Ghost Ranch.

Dinosaurs have been discovered all over Planet Earth. But would you have expected to find their remains near the South Pole? As this illustration shows, Antarctica was once much warmer.

When today's explorers visit Antarctica in the remote southern hemisphere, what they find is a rather bleak and empty landscape. Mostly, it comprises just ice or bare rock, and there is very little by way of plant or animal life. Conditions are harsh, and temperatures often below freezing.

WARMER TIMES

But Antarctica was not always a partly frozen continent. In fact, the climate during Jurassic and Cretaceous times was probably more like that of Great Britain today. This means that, millions of years ago, there would have been lots of animal life, as well as thick forests, in this region of the world.

FORMER SUPERCONTINENT

Antarctica was once part of the supercontinent of Gondwana (GONE-DWAH-NAH). This included South America, India, Africa, and Australia, too, before they broke away and separated. Dinosaurs have been found in all these landmasses. So it is perhaps not entirely surprising that paleontologists have also dug up dinosaur bones in Antarctica.

The first Antarctic find was a Cretaceous ankylosaur, which lived about 80 million years ago. Remains were found on James Ross Island by a group of Argentinian geologists.

Another discovery, made by Dr J. J. Hooker while on an expedition with the British Antarctic Survey, was of a Cretaceous ornithopod.

The ornithopod is related to Hypsilophodon, and has yet to be named. It is currently being studied by experts at the Natural History Musuem, in London.

CRESTED FIND

A third very interesting and much older find dates from Early Jurassic times and has been given the name Cryolophosaurus ellioti (CRY-OL-OFF-OH-SAW-RUS ELL-EE-OH-TEE), which means "Elliot's frozen crested reptile." As you can tell from its name, it seems that this carnivore had a crest on its head which looked rather like that sported by Dilophosaurus, another species of dinosaur dating from around the same period.

Experts are optimistic that further discoveries of dinosaur remains – perhaps of those also found elsewhere – will eventually be made in this part of the world. Perhaps they may even reveal the one-time existence of startlingly different species of dinosaur. The principal problem, however, is the difficulty of digging in the ice and snow, though some have been discovered near the North Pole, too.

Key facts

- Antarctica was not always a mostly frozen wasteland.

- The British Antarctic Survey has helped to unearth dinosaur finds.

- Both herbivores and carnivores have been found in the Antarctic.

Baryonyx

New types of dinosaurs are being discovered all the time. Not long ago, for instance, an amateur fossil-hunter was out in a clay pit near Dorking in Surrey, England, when he came across a strange claw that was sticking out of the mud. No one had ever seen anything like it.

What an amazing discovery! The enormous claw measured all of 12in (30cm) along its outside curve. But Bill Walker, who had unearthed it, was utterly stumped. What sort of creature could possibly have had a claw that size?

Walker turned to the experts but no one could identify the fossil. They, too, were baffled. In fact, scientists from the Natural History Museum in London, led by the paleontologist Alan Charig, were so curious about Walker's discovery that they sent along a team to that very clay pit to see if any more such remains could be found there.

JUST IN TIME

Fortunately they arrived just before a bulldozer had begun to work in the pit. Otherwise, it might have crushed a great many prehistoric bones that were scattered around a small area. What had seemed to be an ordinary clay pit turned out to be a prime site. Walker had struck dinosaur treasure!

All these bones seemed to belong to the same creature; and soon the scientists found they were able to reconstruct almost the whole skeleton of a huge dinosaur.

WALKER'S HEAVY CLAW

Finding so many pieces of a skeleton instead of just fragments was a cause to celebrate. The bones were around 124 million years old, the experts reckoned. What was more, they belonged to a dinosaur that must have looked rather like an Allosaurus, except that it had an unusually narrow snout about 3ft (1m) long, rather like a crocodile's, fairly lengthy front limbs, and extraordinary claws.

Baryonyx *walkeri* was the name they chose for this extraordinary creature, meaning "Walker's heavy claw," after the man who had first found that part of it. Southern England had yielded a most unusual dinosaur indeed.

Key facts

- About half of a complete, fossilized Baryonyx skeleton has been found in southern England.

- Scales and teeth found in its ribcage show that Baryonyx was a fish-eater.

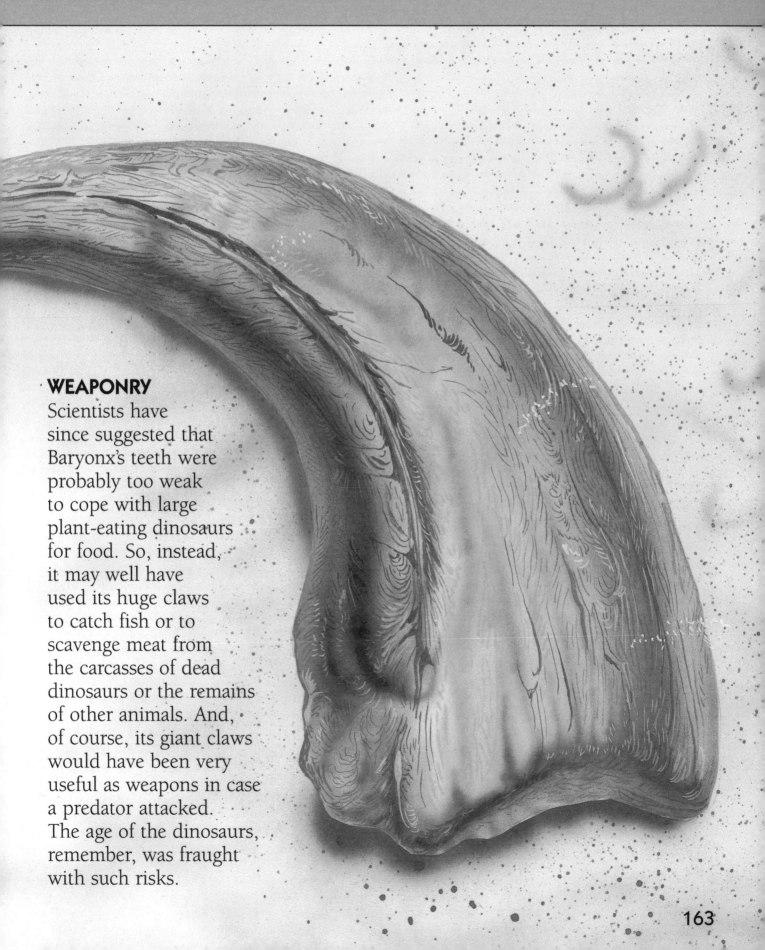

WEAPONRY

Scientists have since suggested that Baryonx's teeth were probably too weak to cope with large plant-eating dinosaurs for food. So, instead, it may well have used its huge claws to catch fish or to scavenge meat from the carcasses of dead dinosaurs or the remains of other animals. And, of course, its giant claws would have been very useful as weapons in case a predator attacked. The age of the dinosaurs, remember, was fraught with such risks.

Monumental

If you are ever in the state of Utah, USA, be sure to visit a large area known as Dinosaur National Monument. The working museum there is a draw for all dinosaur enthusiasts.

By 1915, a great many superb skeletons of herbivores such as Diplodocus, Apatosaurus and Stegosaurus, as well as carnivores like Allosaurus, had been found in the area around the town of Vernal in the state of Utah, USA.

To mark the discoveries of such great dinosaur hunters as Earl Douglass, President Woodrow Wilson of the United States decided that the area should be protected by American law. That was not all: in recognition of all the discoveries that had been made in the region, the whole area, comprising 80 acres, was named Dinosaur National Monument.

WORKING MUSEUM

The quarry there contains one of the largest deposits of dinosaur remains to have been found anywhere in the world. There is even a working museum so that visitors can see the skeletons as they are exposed. Amazingly, remains of almost all the different dinosaurs from Late Jurassic times have been found there.

Key facts

- Dinosaur National Monument is a prime Jurassic site.

- Visitors can view genuine embedded bones there.

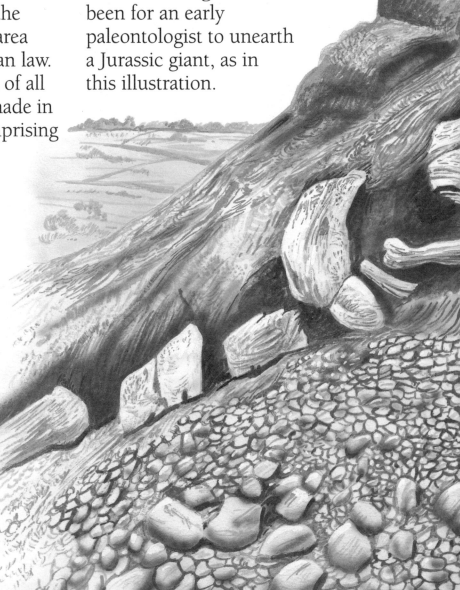

How exciting it must have been for an early paleontologist to unearth a Jurassic giant, as in this illustration.

The story

Fossils are the remains of animals, such as dinosaurs, or plants that lived way back in time. But how exactly are they formed in the ground?

Imagine that, many millions of years ago, a dinosaur – perhaps a Baryonyx – lay dead. It might have died of old age or been unlucky enough to be overcome in combat. Either way, its skeleton would gradually become covered with sand and mud after its flesh had decomposed or been eaten by scavengers. Over millions of years, layers and layers of mud and sand would then build up.

Covering Baryonyx's bones, the lower layers would next slowly turn into rock. Minerals and chemicals would now begin to fill small holes in Baryonyx's bones, making them solid, in a process known as "fossilization."

BREAKTHROUGH

Slowly, too, the layers of rock would start to move a little. Over even more millions of years, as you can see if you follow the sequence of illustrations presented across these two pages, the fossilized bones of Baryonyx would be forced upward, causing the skeleton to break up. Eventually, a claw or some of the bones might come through the surface. Eureka! The fossilized remains of a Baryonyx are about to be discovered!

Sometimes, however, bones and teeth may decompose completely. All that remains is a hole in the rock where they were. Paleontologists call this a *mold*.

# of fossils

Key facts

- Fossils form over a very long period of time, usually millions of years.

- Footprints and droppings can also become fossilized.

- Sometimes fossils form in a mold after the original bones have entirely decomposed.

Various substances can gather inside a mold. These can form a fossil that is made from different materials from the original bones but which will have exactly the same shape. If this occurs, the resulting fossil is known as a *cast*.

JUST A TRACE

Another form of fossil is known as a *trace fossil*. This can be the fossil of a dinosaur's footprint, for example, or even its droppings. (The editor of this encyclopedia has a sizeable lump of fossilized dinosaur droppings on her desk which she uses every day as a paperweight! They are no longer unhygienic, and are thought to have been left behind by an Allosaurus.)

Some types of fossils that have been unearthed have special scientific names which describe their origins. *Ooliths*, for example, are fossilized eggs; *coprolites* are fossilized droppings (these have often provided experts with clues as to what kind of diet the dinosaur enjoyed); and *ichnites* are fossilized tracks.

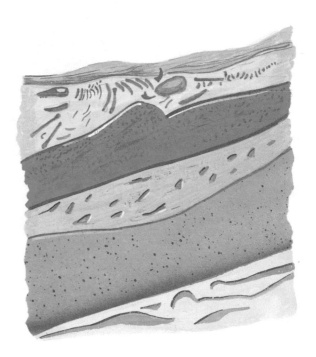

When this bulky dinosaur fossil was discovered over three hundred years ago, the museum curator shown *below* came up with some very strange ideas about the sort of creature it probably came from.

What could it be? Back in the 17th century, Robert Plot, who was a keeper at a museum in Oxford, England, puzzled for ages over an extraordinary, most oddly-shaped fossil that had been dug up from a nearby quarry.

MYSTERY BONE

It was huge, measuring about 2ft (60cm) all around and weighing about 20lb (9kg).

Plot examined it carefully and tried to figure out what sort of creature might have had this bone as part of its anatomy.

At first, he thought it might have been a bone from an elephant. Could such a creature perhaps have been brought to England hundreds of years previously by the Romans? However, there was no evidence at all that the Romans had ever brought elephants to this country.

bone

MISTAKEN IDENTITY

If that was not the case, he decided, it had to be from a member of an extinct race of giant human beings! Now, of course, we know that he was wrong. The wonderful dinosaur fossil, illustrated here, was in fact part of the massive thigh bone of a Megalosaurus! Unfortunately, it has now been lost, but the original drawings of it, made long ago, still exist. At the time when Plot puzzled over the bone, remember, the word *dinosaur* had not even been coined.

Key facts

- Robert Plot first thought what we now know was a Megalosaurus thigh bone came from either an elephant or a giant human being.

- The bone, originally found near Oxford, England, has, unfortunately, since been lost.

Dramatic

In 1978, two American paleontologists unearthed a new species of dinosaur that seems to have been a particularly good mother.

Two eminent scientists – Jack Horner and Robert Makela – happened to be in a fossil store in Montana, USA, when they saw for sale some bones of a baby hadrosaur that had been dug up locally.

LUCKY BREAK
Curious, they asked precisely where the bones came from. Their luck was in, and the two actually managed to find the very nest fairly nearby in some low hills.

Amazingly, what they discovered there were the remains of several other baby dinosaurs in the nest.

What was more, the nest was full of broken pieces of shell, which seemed to indicate that the young dinosaurs had stayed in the nest for some time after hatching, trampling on the remains of the eggs from which they had emerged. There were also signs of vegetation perhaps having been used to line the nest.

Alternatively, it was possible that this vegetation might have been brought to the nest by a parent to feed its young.

discovery

Key facts

- Maiasaura was discovered in Montana, western North America.

- Dinosaurs returned to their nesting grounds year after year.

BABY TEETH

The skeletal remains also showed that the babies had worn-down teeth, a pointer to the fact that they could chew plant food even when still in the nest. Nevertheless, they would have been too young to fend for themselves and so would have been fed by a "good mother dinosaur" or Maiasaura – the name that Horner and Makela gave to the new species of dinosaur they had identified, following that chance discovery in the fossil store.

SIDE BY SIDE

The very next year, a large team of paleontologists visited the site and found many more such remains, which led to that particular spot being named "Egg Mountain." In fact, so many nests have been found in the area that this has led experts to conclude that it must have been inhabited by huge herds of these hadrosaurs back in Cretaceous times. Other species of dinosaur also built nests nearby, so that we can assume they all lived side by side.

discovered

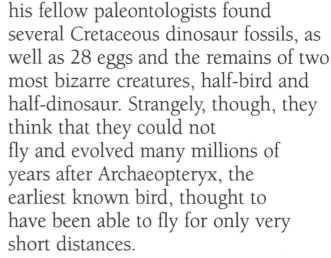

The creature featured here is certainly strange in appearance. What, then, have scientists discovered about this recently-unearthed prehistoric relative of the dinosaurs?

Is it a bird? Is it a dinosaur? No – scientists say it's a dino-bird! Dr Mark Norell of the American Museum of Natural History in New York has come up with a fascinating discovery, following an expedition to the Gobi Desert in Mongolia.

During a dig lasting 10 days, he and his fellow paleontologists found several Cretaceous dinosaur fossils, as well as 28 eggs and the remains of two most bizarre creatures, half-bird and half-dinosaur. Strangely, though, they think that they could not fly and evolved many millions of years after Archaeopteryx, the earliest known bird, thought to have been able to fly for only very short distances.

This dino-bird, which has been named Mononykus (MON-OH-<u>NEYE</u>-KUS), had small wing-like arms only. Scientists are now therefore wondering whether the power of flight was perhaps first developed way back in prehistoric times, only to be lost and then evolve again. Whatever the truth, birds – most scientists now agree – are certainly the distant relations of the dinosaurs.

Key facts

- We now know Velociraptor had a furcula or "wishbone" like a bird, which lends more weight to dinosaurs and birds being related.

Dinosaur

It would certainly be fun to go out to eat in a dinosaur themed restaurant. But just imagine enjoying a meal *inside* a model of a dinosaur!

On New Year's Eve 1853, dinosaur expert Sir Richard Owen gave a most unusual dinner party, held in a British park.

About 20 scientists sat down to enjoy a lavish banquet *inside* an Iguanodon! The meal was delicious. Mock turtle soup was on the menu, followed by a choice of pigeon pie or mutton cutlets.

MODEL MEAL

Never before had any of the scientists eaten in such a strange room. But, of course, this was not a real Iguanodon. Rather, it was a life-sized model, made by the eminent sculptor, Waterhouse Hawkins.

As the dinosaur replica was not quite finished, the guests could sit inside it; and, together, they all drank a toast to the completion of what they thought was an accurate model of Iguanodon.

INACCURATE REPLICA

Sir Richard Owen had told Waterhouse Hawkins what he believed Iguanodon must have looked like when it walked the Earth, but he was not quite right.

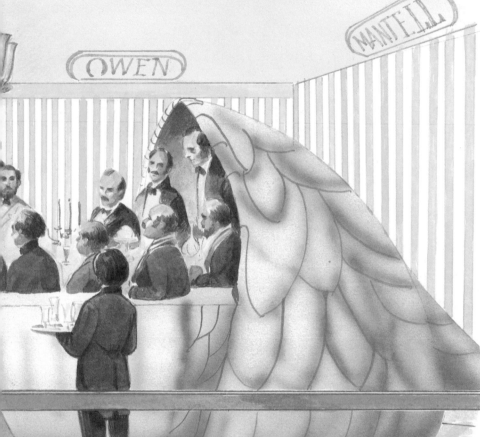
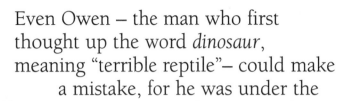

Even Owen – the man who first thought up the word *dinosaur*, meaning "terrible reptile"– could make a mistake, for he was under the impression that Iguanodon must have looked like a giant rhinoceros, with a spike on the end of its nose – which is why Hawkins' model had that strange appearance.

But, of course, we now know that the spike should have been on Iguanodon's hand, and was used by this dinosaur as a weapon.

Many of Waterhouse Hawkins' models still exist today and are on display in the grounds of a park in London, England.

Key facts

- Paleontologist Sir Richard Owen mistook Iguanodon's spiked thumb for a nose horn!

- Sculptor Waterhouse Hawkins made many life-sized models of dinosaurs during the 19th century.

Here are some snippets of exciting news straight from the files of some of the most eminent scientists in the field of paleontology.

Some experts now think that the females of some types of dinosaurs may have been even bigger than the males. This may seem surprising; but, in fact, among today's reptiles, the females are also frequently larger and more robust.

Another strange piece of dinosaur news involves a missing 120-million-year-old footprint, like the one *below right*, that has disappeared from the Isle of Wight, off the southern coast of England. It was a 18in (45cm)-long Iguanodon track; and scientists think that it must have been cut out of the rock by thieves. The best of three such prints discovered, it was visible only when the tide was out. Now, sadly, no one is able to view this interesting dinosaur trace fossil anymore.

ANOTHER T REX

Tyrannosaurus rex is probably the most famous of all the dinosaurs; yet only about a dozen or so nearly complete skeletons of this prehistoric monster have been dug up so far.

Now, however, another has been discovered that is a fifth larger than the previous record. It was discovered by volunteers digging up a prehistoric river bed in Hell Creek, Montana, USA.

In 1997, too, the Field Museum, Chicago, USA, acquired at an auction a Tyrannosaurus (good-humoredly nicknamed Sue) after it had been the subject of dispute over ownership between members of the Sioux tribe and the team of paleontologists who dug it up.

Key facts

- The oldest dinosaur eggs containing embryos were discovered near Lisbon, Portugal, in June 1997.

- A new species of dinosaur is discovered about every seven weeks. This makes paleontology a very exciting science.

discoveries

HIGH PRICES

Dinosaur bones and eggs are now fetching high prices, particularly in the United States and Japan. Private dealers as well as fossil shops, are offering them for sale; and sometimes they come up at auctions. One American catalog lists fossil specimens priced at several thousand dollars; and some skeletons will fetch millions.

Paleontologists are concerned that important sites may be raided for the money that such remains may bring. That is why some countries have decided to ban the export of fossils so that they at least stay in that part of the world where they were dug up. To meet the demand for fossilized remains, some companies are now making replicas.

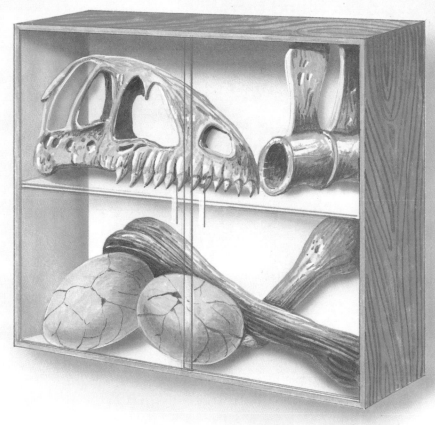

COSMIC CATASTROPHE

Physicists working at the Israeli Space Research Institute in Haifa, Israel, have come up with an idea about the mass extinction of all the dinosaurs 65 million years ago.

According to Professor Arnon Dar, they think that the destruction of these huge beasts may have been caused by the collision of two stars. This would have created a massive wave of cosmic radiation, destroying the protective layer of our planet's atmosphere so that life on Earth was widely obliterated. Apparently, every single day, twin stars merge in the same way somewhere in the Universe; but fortunately most are much too far away from Earth to do any harm.

Some sites discovered by paleontologists are known as "dinosaur graveyards" because a great number of bones, including whole skeletons, have been found there.

Remains can, of course, be discovered completely by chance. But, in most cases, paleontologists set out on an expedition to a fossil site and will start by looking for fragments of bone. Such a site may be at the foot of cliffs, in quarries, by river banks or in deserts in remote parts of the world. Here, the type and age of exposed rock may indicate that there might be rich dinosaur pickings from a veritable "dinosaur graveyard."

SAFETY FIRST

But such locations are frequently fraught with potential danger and so it is never wise to go on a fossil-hunting trip unless it is properly supervised. In fact, it is sometimes possible for student and adult amateurs to join one.

Even if you personally did not face danger during the excavation, unless given specific instructions you could damage any remains you found while trying to remove them. That is something to be avoided at all costs: such valuable prehistoric finds cannot, after all, be replaced.

Key facts

- Experts can now calculate the age of fossil-bearing rocks by measuring the level of their radioactivity. This will, in turn, give the approximate age of any dinosaur bones found in that location.

Experts

A paleontologist stands proudly with a fossil find. But how was the bone unearthed? What exactly is involved in digging for dinosaurs?

True fossil-hunters never just start digging unsystematically. If they worked haphazardly, the chances are that any bones would become dislodged and then break up. Rather, they have to proceed slowly and patiently in teams, sometimes spending hours on end just brushing away layers of sand.

Other instances, however – when perhaps a skeleton is virtually entombed – may call for very careful use of drills or maybe even explosives.

DIG THIS!
Now the delicate work of actually freeing the fossils can begin. Mostly, it will be necessary to remove them while they are still encased in huge blocks of rock. Some will need special protection in plaster and sacking to ensure they do not disintegrate.

LISTING EVERYTHING
At this point, cataloging and photographing the exposed bones can begin. This will help experts reconstruct the skeleton back at the museum to which the remains are taken. Everything found has to be very carefully listed.

All parts of the dinosaur that have been dug up – teeth, skull, vertebrae, legs, feet and tail – will need to be studied in detail and may be written up in a scientific paper. And, of course, the dinosaur will have to be named, as described on page 188, if it is a new species.

JOINING FORCES
Will the find perhaps be an entirely new type of dinosaur? That is the most exciting prospect of all. Most of the paleontological institutions cooperate very closely throughout the world and share information about discoveries, thereby adding to the international scientific data bank on dinosaurs.

IN STORE
There are occasions, however, when so many bones – sometimes hundreds of tons of them – are unearthed in the course of a dig that they simply have to be stored away, having been labeled first, because not enough room can be found to put them on public view.

Key facts
- Paleontologists often paint resin on crumbly fossils to stop them from breaking up as they are unearthed, thereby preserving them.

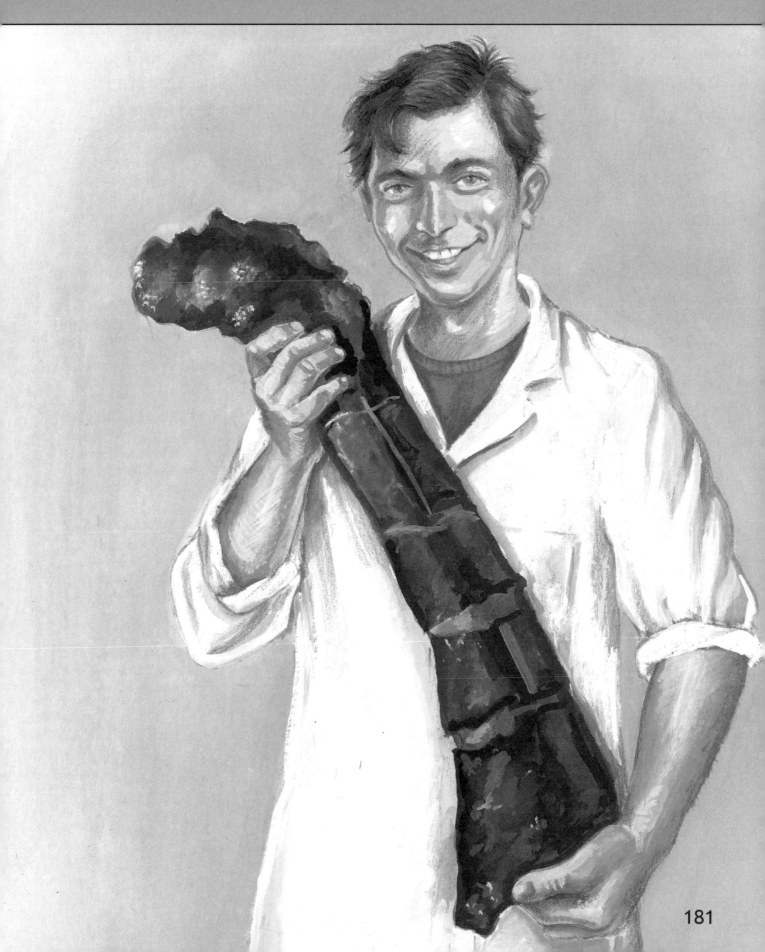

There are dinosaur skeletons on view in many natural history museums throughout the world. A great deal of preparation had to be done before such remains were ready for reconstruction and final display.

When a museum is sent the fossilized bones of one or more dinosaurs after a dig, the very first job is to find somewhere to store them safely. There may be hundreds or even thousands of bones to sort and study. All will have been labeled when excavated, and there will also be accompanying sketches of their original positions to help with later reconstruction.

CHIPPING AWAY

The next stage is to take them out of their packaging very carefully to avoid any damage. Now the bones have to be removed from the casing of rock in which they are embedded. This is carried out using a variety of instruments, ranging from small needles and chisels to machines that blow air at the rock.

laboratory

A microscope can help with this, particularly if bones are fragile. You can see one being used in this illustration.

CAREFUL TREATMENT

Sometimes the bones have to be treated with special chemicals to preserve them. After having been buried in the ground for many millions of years, they can easily become damaged by exposure to the air and through rough handling. Eventually, the specimens are ready for illustration and description. Then they can be compared with other remains and identified if there is doubt. Next time you see a dinosaur in a museum, consider the many months and perhaps years of painstaking work that will have gone on behind the scenes.

Key facts

- Scientists can usually assess when a dinosaur lived by dating the rock strata in which it has been found.

- Scans have been used in the laboratory to look inside unhatched dinosaur eggs and view the fossilized embryos that never hatched.

Reconstructing

Putting together a dinosaur's skeleton helps paleontologists build up a profile of that particular prehistoric creature's lifestyle.

The first step in rebuilding a dinosaur skeleton is for all the bones to be laid out in the correct order. If paleontologists are in doubt about this, they will look very carefully at the skeletons of other similar dinosaurs and assess where the vertebrae and other bones should go.

Some large skeletons that are on display in museums today are actually fiberglass replicas, made using rubber molds of remains. These are lightweight and rather easier to put together than the original bones. Sometimes, too, fiberglass is merely used to replace any of the bones that are missing.

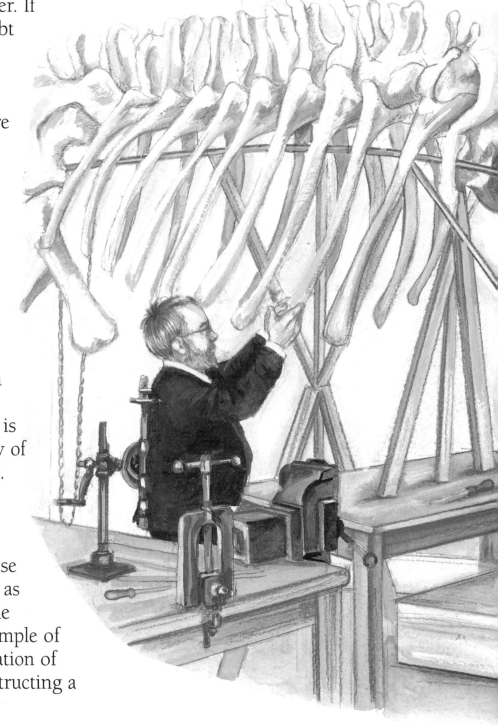

TAKING SHAPE

To help put a skeleton together, paleontologists use a steel framework, known as an *armature*, to support the bones. You can see an example of an armature in this illustration of experts at work on reconstructing a long-necked dinosaur.

dinosaurs

Key facts

- Some museums have robotic dinosaurs on display. These are built after careful study of the original skeletons, and can move and roar.

IN SUSPENSE

Some dinosaurs are reconstructed in another way, however. The bones are suspended from the ceiling, so that they look much like a very large puppet, rather than being supported from below.

DETECTIVE WORK

From the reconstructed skeleton, scientists can then start to work out whether the dinosaur was bipedal or walked on all-fours; whether it was a herbivore or carnivore; and how athletic it might have been. All in all, it is like a giant piece of detective work.

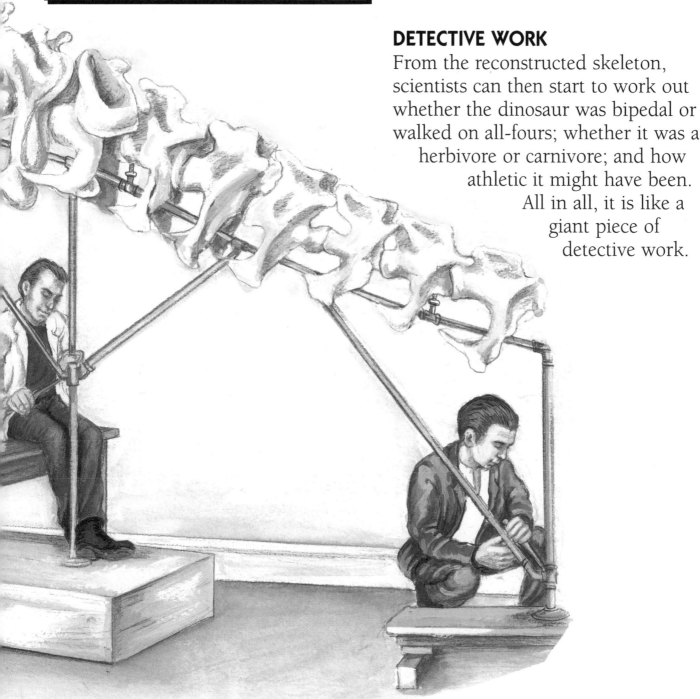

How wonderful it would be if only scientists could find a way of recreating some of the various types of dinosaurs that once existed! How could they possibly set about this?

If you have seen the film *Jurassic Park*, you'll know that the story is about a group of scientists who create a sensational dinosaur park on a remote Pacific island. They do this by using DNA from the blood of an insect that was trapped in amber, or fossilized sap, back in Jurassic times, 150 million years ago. The recreation of prehistoric life in this way is something that some paleontologists agree may be possible in theory.

BACK FROM EXTINCTION

In *Jurassic Park*, the insect, when alive, happened to have bitten a dinosaur. This meant that there was dinosaur DNA in the insect and that this DNA could be used by scientists to recreate living dinosaurs millions of years *after* they became extinct.

If scientists wanted to bring back dinosaurs from extinction, they would first need to get hold of dinosaur DNA in some way, and then begin growing it in living cells.

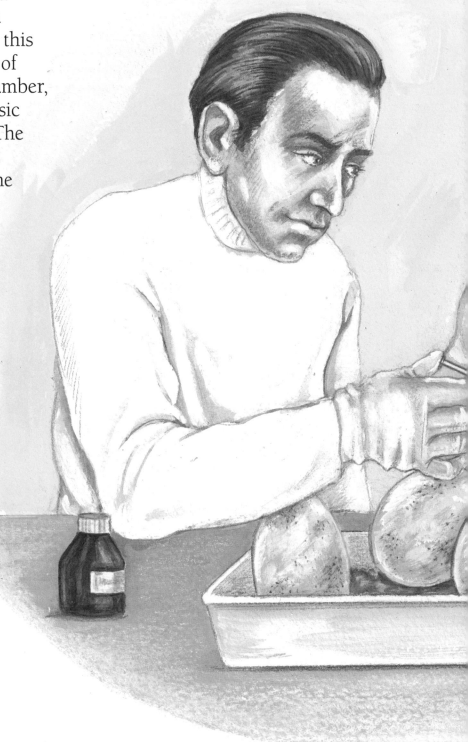

to life

CRACKING IT

Dinosaurs' closest living relatives are birds. So the most logical creature to work with would be the largest type of bird – something like an ostrich.

Having obtained DNA from a male and female of the same type of dinosaur, scientists might try injecting it into ostrich eggs. When these eggs hatched, all the chicks would be ostriches but some, with luck, would perhaps have dinosaur "sex" cells.

FUTURE SHOCK

After the ostrich chicks grew into adults and mated, the females would lay eggs. When these hatched, some would be ostriches, but some *might* be dinosaurs! What a shock it would be to find that the events recounted in *Jurassic Park* actually foretold the future!

Key facts

- DNA is a sort of code in the cells of all living things. It is this special code that causes the young of any creatures to grow up to look like their parents.

- Minute traces of DNA may still exist in some fossilized dinosaur bones, if only we could identify which and then extract it.

Dinosaur names are sometimes quite difficult to pronounce until you get the hang of them. But who actually gives these creatures their names as new ones are unearthed, and how are the names chosen?

Dinosaurs are most often named after the person who sponsored the expedition during which they were discovered, or the paleontologist who made the find. Many dinosaurs have also been given names with a Latin or Greek origin and which describe their size or some special body part.

A PTERODACTYL CALLED ARTHUR

Recently, though, a number of scientists have become rather more adventurous when naming dinosaurs. A new pterodactyl, for example, has been named after the 19th-century author Sir Arthur Conan Doyle. (Doyle was very interested in dinosaurs during his lifetime, and even wrote a novel in which they feature.)

The splendid new pterodactyl, found in Brazil and with a wingspan of 21ft (6m), has been named Arthurdactylus conan-doylei (ARTHUR-DAKT-EE LOSS CONE-AN-DOY-LAY). Shown *above*, it is now in the Natural History Museum, Karlsruhe, Germany.

STAR NAMES

Steven Spielberg, director of the movie *Jurassic Park*, recently sponsored a dig in China. One of the finds was an ankylosaur from Jurassic times. They named it Tianchiasaurus (TEE-AN-CHEE-A-SAW-RUS), which means "heavenly lizard," but also gave it a second name – nedegoaperferima (NED-EGG-OH-AP-ERF-ERRY-MAH) – so that its full title is Tianchiasaurus nedegoaperferima.

This second name has no meaning but is made up from letters taken from the surnames of some of the stars in the movie – Sam <u>Ne</u>ill, Laura <u>Der</u>n, Jeff <u>Gol</u>dblum, Richard <u>At</u>tenborough, Bob <u>Pec</u>k, Martin <u>Fe</u>rero, Ariana <u>Ric</u>hards and Jospeh <u>Ma</u>zello.

A CARVE-UP

But one of the strangest dinosaur names of all must be Irritator (EE-RIT-<u>ART</u>-OR). The story behind this name, given to an Early Cretaceous theropod from Brazil, is a curious one. It seems unscrupulous fossil-dealers in Brazil have been known to carve remains into more interesting shapes simply to get more money for them. One was even carved to look as if it had come from a pterosaur; but experts later found out what had been done to the fossil.

They also realised that it was in fact from a new type of theropod. So angry were they at how the dealer had damaged the remains that they have given the new dinosaur the name of *Irritator*, meaning "annoying"!

CHOOSE A NAME

Imagine the dinosaur *below* had to be given a name. What would you choose to call it, and why?

Dinosaurs ruled for more than 150 million years, and their remains have been discovered on every continent, as you will discover for yourself in a fact-packed section devoted to dinosaur geography.

Around 220 million years ago, in Late Triassic times when dinosaurs first appeared on this planet, the world looked entirely different from the way it does today. Originally, there was just one main landmass that scientists have named Pangaea, meaning "all Earth," which was completely surrounded by seas. Over many millions of years, however, this supercontinent began to split into two main parts. We know these today as Laurasia (LAW-RACE-EAR) and Gondwana.

CONTINENTAL DRIFT
By about 145 million years ago, in Late Jurassic times, many new dinosaurs had evolved and the two great land masses had slowly drifted farther apart. But what is now North America was still joined to Europe and Asia at that time; and what are now South America and Africa had not yet separated either. Not until Late Cretaceous times did the continents form and begin to take on the sort of positions that they have today.

The same type of dinosaur unearthed in one part of the world has also sometimes been dug up far away. This is because, at various stages in the globe's history before the continents had separated, dinosaurs could migrate over huge distances.

There may even have been land bridges that dinosaurs used to cross over large areas of sea – perhaps from Asia to North America, for instance, or in other directions.

atlas

But certain other dinosaurs from later periods have been discovered in one area only. Quite simply, they may have become cut off from the rest of the globe by deep oceans that had begun to form barriers to their wanderings.

Fearsome predators like Tyrannosaurus rex and gigantic herbivores – gentle unless provoked – such as Triceratops, as well as the squawking pterosaurs that soared the prehistoric skies above them, are among the best-known creatures from the age of the dinosaurs. You can see them in this illustration.

But, in all, over five hundred different types of dinosaur have been found to date, and there may be many more just waiting to be unearthed.

Areas that are rich in dinosaur remains have two main things in common. Firstly, heat and pressure from the Earth's interior have not crushed or melted the fossils in that region. And secondly, the rock in which the fossils have formed dates from 220-65 million years ago, when dinosaurs roamed our planet. Cliffs, quarries and desert sands – all have yielded fascinating dinosaur bones, as well as fossilized nests and eggs.

DINOSAUR TOUR

But where have most dinosaur discoveries been made? As you study the pictorial maps on the pages that follow, you will discover the sites where many dinosaurs that you perhaps recognize and know something about already have been dug up. But there are bound to be many of these prehistoric creatures that are completely new to you, too.

Amazingly, fresh finds are being made as often as every few weeks. So could there perhaps be an entirely new species waiting to be discovered somewhere in *your* neighborhood? What an exciting thought! Read on, and you will soon become an expert in dinosaur geography in your own right.

Dug up

Join us as we take a look at some of the principal dinosaurs that once roamed what is now Europe. All those millions of years ago, remember, Great Britain would have been part of the mainland.

Great Britain is in fact the perfect place to start our world dinosaur tour. After all, it was here that the word *dinosaur* was first used in 1842 by the great paleontologist Sir Richard Owen to describe these prehistoric creatures. He coined the term by taking two Greek words – *deinos* (meaning "terrible") and *sauros* (meaning "lizard") – and combining them. Together with the sculptor Waterhouse Hawkins, Owen also produced the first life-sized models of dinosaurs which were put on public display.

Chance finds

Several European dinosaur discoveries have occured entirely by accident. The remains of lots of Iguanodon, for example, were discovered by coal-miners in Belgium; while an amateur fossil-hunter named Bill Walker came across the fossilized claw of a Baryonyx while he was rummaging around in a clay pit in Surrey, England.

Remains of Saltopus (SALT-OH-PUSS), 1, a very small carnivore, have been unearthed in Scotland, in the very north of Great Britain. Most dinosaur discoveries, however, have been made farther south. Among them are Megalosaurus, 2, a fearsome predator that would have terrified many smaller creatures in this region; and the large plant-eater Iguanodon, 3, famous for its spiked thumbs, and also dug up on mainland Europe.

MAINLAND DISCOVERIES
Some of the earliest dinosaurs of all have been found on the mainland of Europe. The primitive predator Procompsognathus, 5, lived in what is now Germany, for instance; and Plateosaurus (PLAT-EE-OH-SAW-RUS), 4, also from Triassic times but a plant-eater, roamed western Europe, too. Compsognathus (COMP-SOG-NAY-THUS), 7, a tiny Jurassic flesh-eater, has been found in France and Germany; and, millions of years later, in Cretaceous times, Hypsilophodon, 8, – a small, speedy plant-eater – roamed what is now Spain and Portugal, as well as the territory now known as Great Britain.

Eggs, nests, dinosaur footprints and other trace fossils have also been found at a number of sites throughout the whole of western Europe and have been put on display in all the major natural history museums there.

in Europe

Eastern Europe – including Russia, Poland and Romania, for instance – has yielded fascinating dinosaur remains, too, including what may possibly be a relative of Psittacosaurus, **6**, a Cretaceous herbivore with a parrot-like beak, found in China and Mongolia.

KEY

1 Saltopus

2 Megalosaurus

3 Iguanodon

4 Plateosaurus

5 Procompsognathus

6 Psittacosaurus-like dinosaur

7 Compsognathus

8 Hypsilophodon

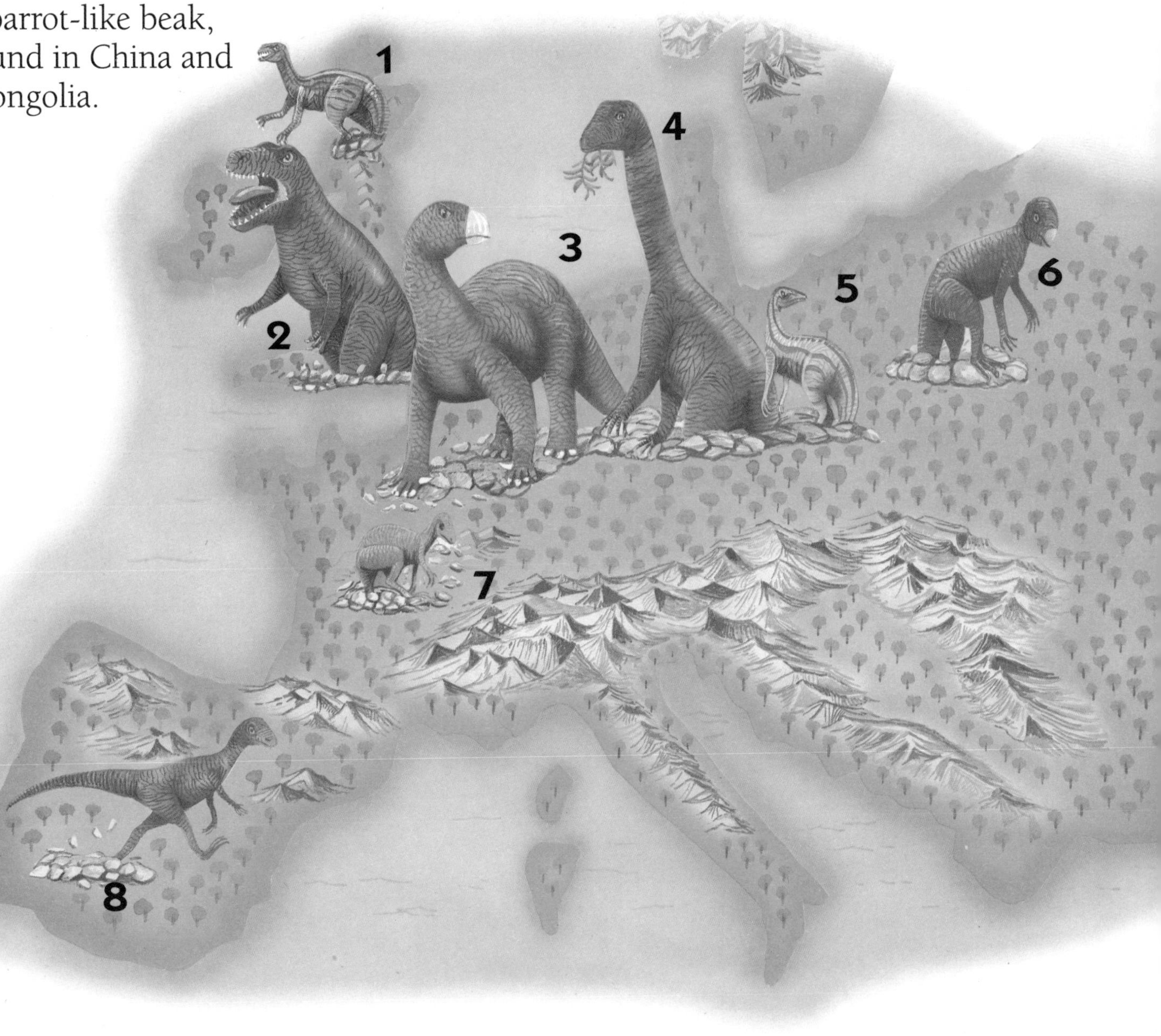

Remote parts of China and Mongolia may not have much animal life today; but way back in prehistoric times, these regions – and possibly other parts of Asia – seem to have been inhabited by a huge variety of carnivores and herbivores.

In all, around one hundred different types of dinosaurs, as well as fossilized eggs and nests, have been found in China alone. So there is only room for a few of the main finds on our map. See if you can spot Lufengosaurus (LOO-FENG-OH-SAW-RUS), **4**, a large plant-eater; Mamenchisaurus (MAM-EN-KEY-SAW-RUS), **3**, the dinosaur with the longest neck; Shunosaurus (SHOO-NOH-SAW-RUS), **2**, a large four-footed plant-eater with a long tail ending, unusually, in a bony club; and Microceratops (MY-CROW-SER-A-TOPS), **9**, a tiny herbivore with a beak and small neck frill.

MONGOLIAN REMAINS

In Mongolia, too, there have been lots of interesting dinosaur discoveries. Among the most well-known of these are Oviraptor, **12**, a curious crested predator with a name meaning 'egg thief'; and Protoceratops, **11**, a small plant-eater with a bony neck frill. What is now the Gobi Desert, in Mongolia, was also home to Gallimimus, **1**, an ostrich-like, fast-running theropod.

Pinacosaurus (PEA-NAK-OH-SAW-RUS), **8**, a 17ft (5m)-long armored plant-eater with a tail club that was ideal for swiping at enemies, lived in Mongolia, too, as did Velociraptor, **10**, a most ferocious predator, even though small by dinosaur standards.

INSIDE INDIA

In India, meanwhile, paleontologists have dug up the bones of Indosuchus (IND-OH-SOOK-US), **7**, a smaller version of fearsome Tyrannosaurus rex; Barapasaurus (BA-RAP-A-SAW-RUS), **5**, a long-necked herbivore with a name meaning 'big leg lizard'; and also a smaller, plated dinosaur, known as Dravidosaurus (DRA-VID-OH-SAW-RUS), **6**, that had a magnificent spiked tail for warding off predators.

As for other parts of Asia, there have only been a few discoveries in Japan and Korea, for example, so far; but it could be that this continent still harbors many dinosaur secrets for scientists to unearth.

Dragon bones

In some parts of China, dinosaur bones were once thought to belong to dragons. Some people even believed that, if ground up, these bones had medicinal properties and could be used to cure all sorts of illnesses and diseases.

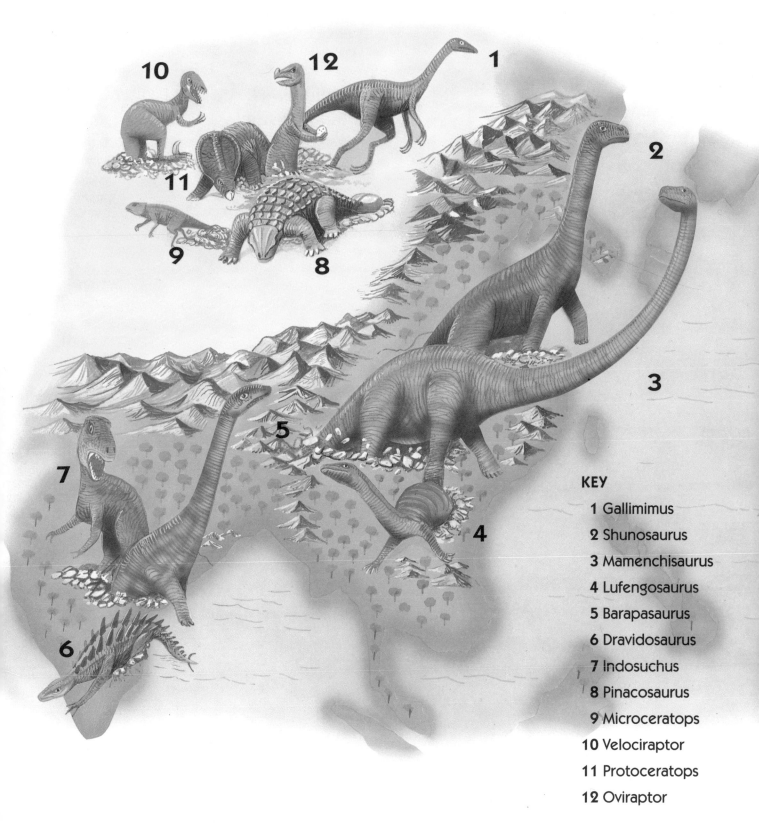

KEY

1 Gallimimus

2 Shunosaurus

3 Mamenchisaurus

4 Lufengosaurus

5 Barapasaurus

6 Dravidosaurus

7 Indosuchus

8 Pinacosaurus

9 Microceratops

10 Velociraptor

11 Protoceratops

12 Oviraptor

Canada and the United States have so far yielded more dinosaur discoveries than anywhere else in the world – over 170 different types in all, dating from Triassic times, when dinosaurs first evolved, right through to their extinction 65 million years ago.

More and more exciting new finds are being made in Canada and the United States – so many, in fact, that there is only room to illustrate a few of the most famous and varied on our pictorial map. Dinosaur Provincial Park, for example, in Alberta, Canada, is so named because it is a haven for paleontologists.

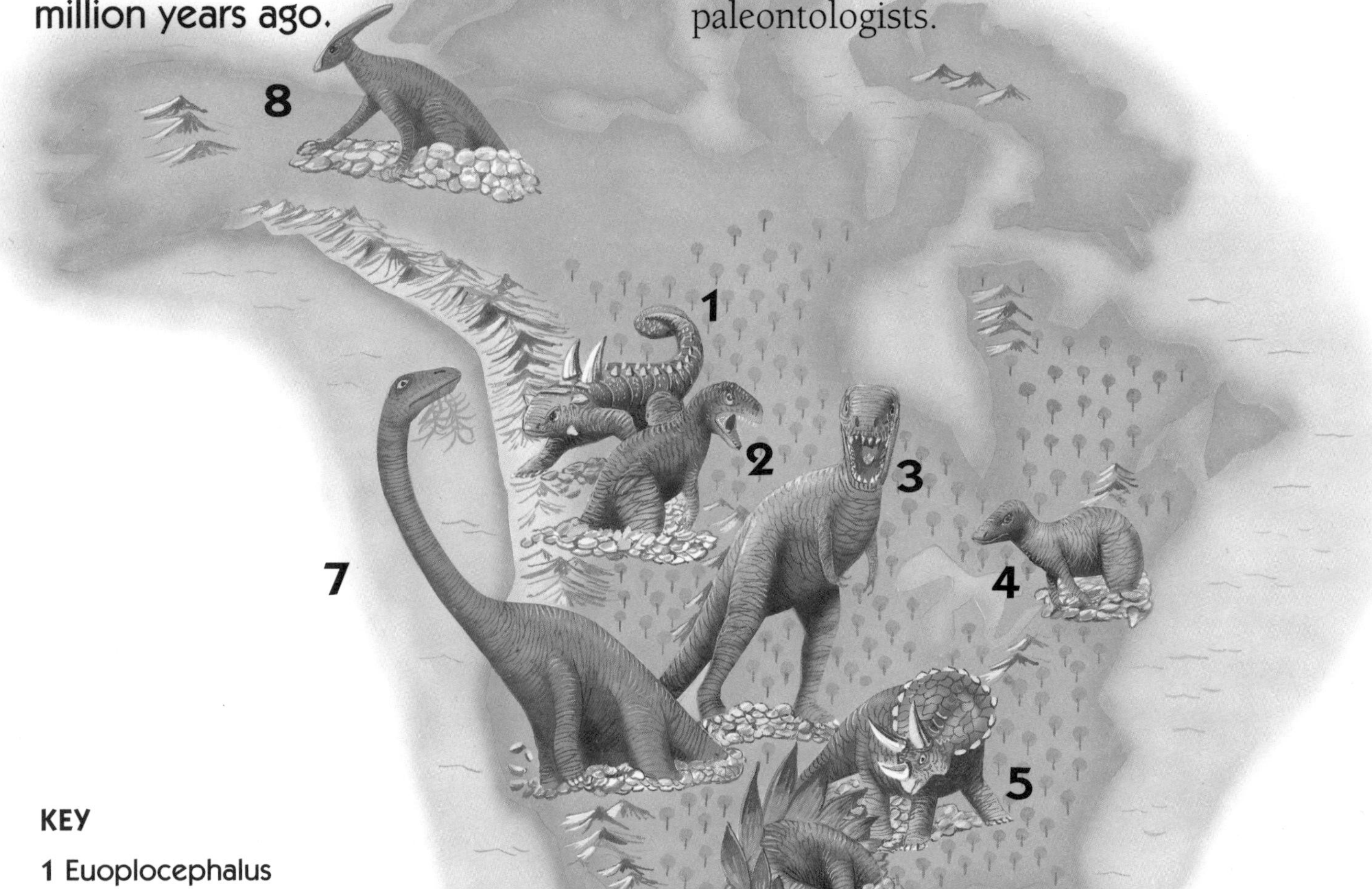

KEY

1 Euoplocephalus

2 Albertosaurus

3 Tyrannosaurus rex

4 Hadrosaurus

5 Triceratops

6 Stegosaurus

7 Diplodocus

8 Parasaurolophus

Among the discoveries there have been Albertosaurus (AL-BERT-OH-SAW-RUS), **2**, a giant two-ton carnivore that is named after the region; and Euoplocephalus, **1**, an enormous armored ankylosaur, which had a spiky head.

Canada was also home to hadrosaurs, horned dinosaurs and bone-heads. Excavations began there back in the 1880s; and within thirty years, the great dinosaur hunter Barnum Brown had begun collecting specimens on behalf of the American Museum of Natural History and the Canadian Geological Survey. There is even evidence that huge herds of thousands of dinosaurs, once drowned in terrible floods in what is now Canada.

NATIONAL MONUMENT

In the American state of Utah, meanwhile, is the Dinosaur National Monument. Here, paleontologists have dug up the long-necked dinosaur Diplodocus, **7**, and plated Stegosaurus, **6**. Major North American finds also include Parasaurolophus, **8**, the plant-eater with a magnificent hollow tube on its head through which it could bellow, and Tyrannosaurus rex, **3**, surely among the very fiercest of all prehistoric monsters and known to have suffered from gout because of all the meat it ate.

Triceratops, **5**, the three-horned herbivore, and the duck-billed plant-eater Hadrosaurus, **4**, also feature prominently among American finds.

It was thanks to such philanthropists as Andrew Carnegie that many early American discoveries were made. He even had one named after him – Diplodocus carnegiei. And another massive long-neck was named after his wife – Apatasaurus louisae.

Most North American discoveries have, of course, been made in desert-like regions where fossil sites became exposed by weathering. It is just as likely, however, that there might be remains under the prairies, forests or major cities. What excavations at such places might ultimately reveal, we shall probably never know.

Making their mark

Geologists working in Mexico, which links North and South America, have found evidence for an enormous meteorite that must have hit Earth many millions of years ago. The impact was so great that it left the deepest of craters, still visible today. Could this collision, scientists wonder, have contributed to the demise of the dinosaurs at least on the North American continent, if not South America and elsewhere, too?

The continent of Africa comprises an enormous landmass, so it is perhaps not surprising that lots of interesting dinosaur remains have been discovered there.

What an amazing find it was! Over a period of four years in the early 20th century, German paleontologist Werner Janensch and his team unearthed, at a remote place called Tendaguru in Tanzania, over 200 tons of fossilized bones – the remains of dinosaurs thought to have died millions of years ago in a great flood. Among them were the herbivores Brachiosaurus, **2**, Barosaurus (BARROW-SAW-RUS), **3**, and Dicraeosaurus (DICK-REYE-OH-SAW-RUS), **7**, as well as carnivorous Ceratosaurus-like dinosaurs, **6**. A gigantic rebuilt skeleton of a Brachiosaurus that was found there is now on public view in a museum in Berlin, Germany.

HEADLESS SKELETON
Another Jurassic plant-eater, Vulcanodon, **5**, was found in the African country of Zimbabwe in 1972. But, alas, its skeleton was not complete. The entire head was missing for some mysterious reason, so scientists, by comparing it with other sauropods, had to imagine what this part of its body must have been like.

Meanwhile, in South Africa, the bones of another four-footed plant-eater Massospondylus (MASS-OH-SPOND-EE-LUS), **4**, have been discovered; and in Egypt, and later in Niger, the remains of the 15ft (4m)-long, two-legged, sail-backed predator Spinosaurus, **1**, were dug up. Beneath the sands in Niger, too, were found the bones of an Ouranosaurus, **8**, also sail-backed but a plant-eater.

More recently, in 1995, in Morocco, the skull of an enormous carnivore was unearthed. This belonged to a dinosaur that experts have chosen to name Carcharodontosaurus (KARK-ARROW-DONT-OH-SAW-RUS), **9**. But the story of Africa's dinosaurs does not have to end here, for paleontologists believe there are probably many more discoveries to be made in this part of the world.

Massive dig

The excavations at Tendaguru in Tanzania took place between 1909 and 1912. So many dinosaur remains were dug up here that workers were involved in over 5,000 return journeys to the nearest port in order to ship all the fossils to Germany, from where the expedition had begun. The excavation yielded more remains than any on this continent since.

Africa

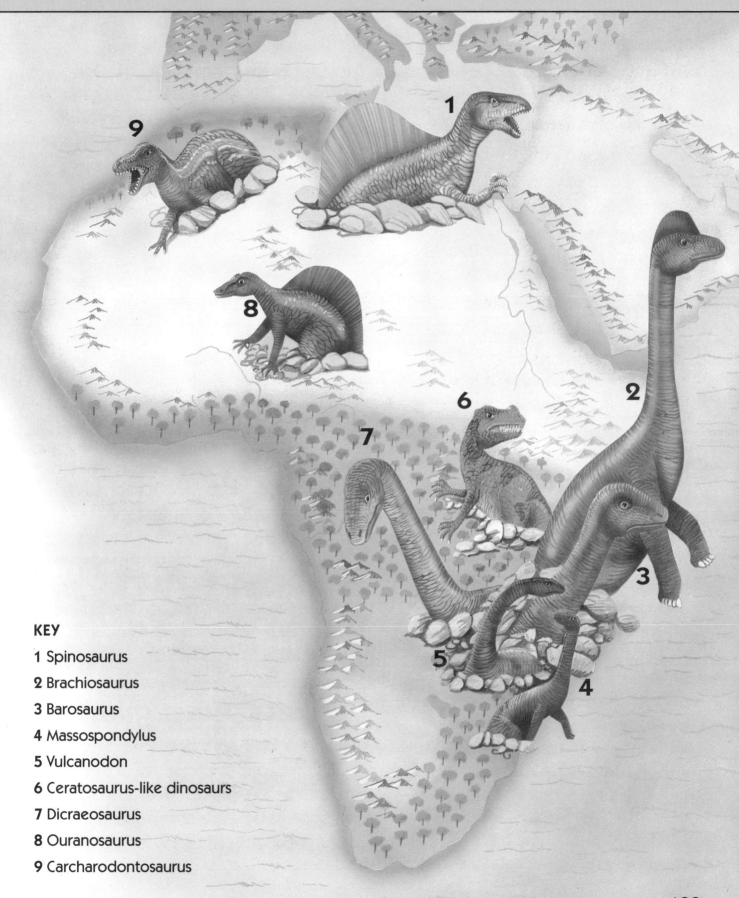

KEY

1 Spinosaurus

2 Brachiosaurus

3 Barosaurus

4 Massospondylus

5 Vulcanodon

6 Ceratosaurus-like dinosaurs

7 Dicraeosaurus

8 Ouranosaurus

9 Carcharodontosaurus

South American

Some of the world's very first and most unusual dinosaurs have been unearthed in countries such as Argentina and Brazil, as well as Bolivia and Venezuela.

As you can see from this map, most dinosaur fossils found in South America have been discovered in desert and grassland regions. There could, of course, also be remains under the South American continent's thick, tropical vegetation; but it is difficult to dig for them in such areas and preferable to leave the jungle undisturbed, so we may never know.

EARLY CARNIVORES

One of the earliest dinosaurs of all has been found in South America. This was Staurikosaurus (STOR-ICK-OH-SAW-RUS), 3, a 6ft (2m)-long carnivore from southern Brazil. Of course, it was not anywhere near the size of the later giant meat-eaters, but it still would have been greatly feared by the prey it stalked.

Herrerasaurus (HAIR-AIR-OH-SAW-RUS), 10, another early carnivore that must have been about 10ft (3m) long, was found in north-west Argentina, as was small 3ft (90cm)-long Pisanosaurus (PEA-SAN-OH-SAW-RUS), 4, an herbivore known only from a few fragments of bone and teeth.

The skeletal remains of a baby Mussaurus, 6, meanwhile, a Triassic herbivore, have been found together with some of its eggshell in central Argentina. Its parents, too, would have been dwarfed by Riojasaurus (REE-OK-A-SAW-RUS), 2, another four-legged early herbivore reaching 36ft (11m)in length. Later remains have also been found in Argentina. Most well-known are Piatnitzkysaurus (PEA-AT-NITS-KY-SAW-RUS), 7, a two-legged carnivore, and Patagosaurus (PAT-AG-OH-SAW-RUS), 5, a large herbivore.

STRANGE BUT TRUE

Two long-necked plant-eaters from South America – Titanosaurus (TIE-TAN-OH-SAW-RUS), 9, and Saltasaurus (SALT-A-SAW-RUS), 1 – seem to have had protruding lumps of bone for additional body protection, a most unusual feature among sauropods. Strange, too, was the 25ft (7.5m)-long Argentinian carnivore Carnotaurus; 8, with its bull-like horns and remarkably bumpy skin.

Cretaceous giant

Hot news from Argentina is the discovery of a Cretaceous carnivore that experts have named Giganotosaurus (JEYE-GAN-OT-OH-SAW-RUS) because of its gigantic size – all of about 40ft (12.5m) in length.

safari

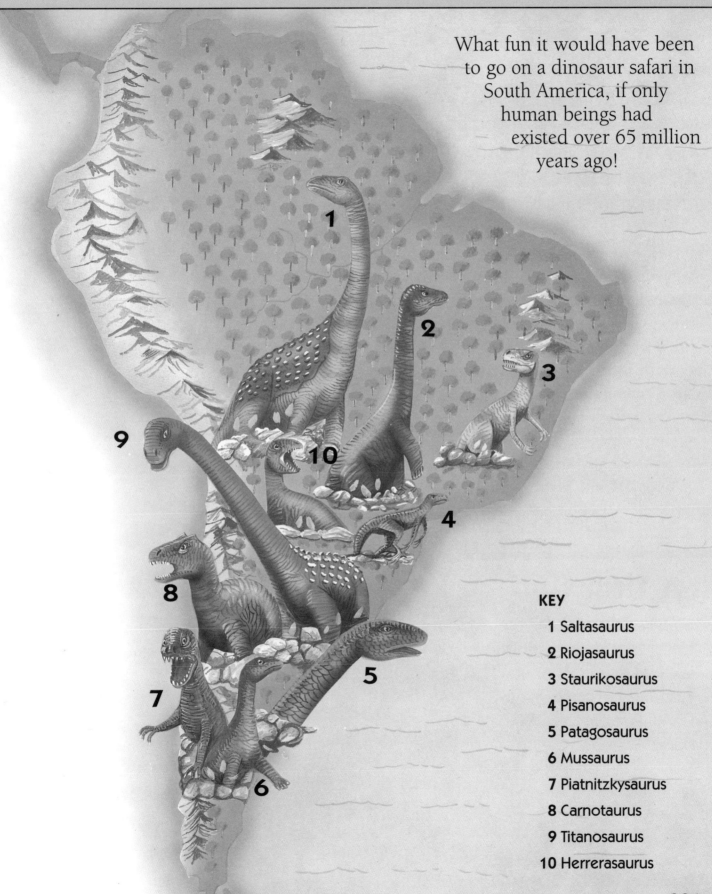

What fun it would have been to go on a dinosaur safari in South America, if only human beings had existed over 65 million years ago!

KEY

1 Saltasaurus

2 Riojasaurus

3 Staurikosaurus

4 Pisanosaurus

5 Patagosaurus

6 Mussaurus

7 Piatnitzkysaurus

8 Carnotaurus

9 Titanosaurus

10 Herrerasaurus

Remains from

So far, very few dinosaurs have been discovered on the vast continent of Australia. However, there are lots of fossilized tracks at what were probably the sites of dinosaur stampedes, so many remains may still lie buried.

In 1980, Australia's first armored plant-eater, **3**, was dug up in Queensland. Scientists named it Minmi (MIN-MEE). Another important find, meanwhile, has been the herbivore Muttaburrasaurus, **1**, with its marvelous spiked thumbs. The rather smaller plant-eater Leaellynosaurus (LEE-LYE-NOH-SAW-RUS), **4**, is a more recent discovery from the state of Victoria.

A firm find

Among recent Australian discoveries is a small, four-legged Cretaceous plant-eater that has been identified from just a jaw bone. Atlascopcosaurus (AT-LASS-COP-COH-SAW-RUS) has been named after the Atlas Copco Corporation helping to ecavate it.

This dinosaur was named after a girl called Leaellyn. She often accompanied her parents when they went on expeditions to hunt for dinosaur fossils. Just imagine how exciting it must be to have a dinosaur named after you!

down under

AUSTRALIAN PREDATORS

But it seems that the land mass that is now Australia was not only home to various species of herbivores.

Indeed, the oldest dinosaur discovered there so far – Agrosaurus (AGG-ROH-SAW-RUS), **2**, dating from Triassic times – probably ate insects and small animals, as well as plants. Such fearsome carnivores as Allosaurus, **5**, more usually associated with North America, roamed here, too; while the shinbone of a smaller Australian predator was given the name Kakuru (KAK-OO-ROO), **6**, meaning "rainbow serpent" because its remains had become shiny as they fossilized.

FUTURE FINDS

As yet, there have been hardly any discoveries of dinosaurs in Tasmania and New Zealand, to the south of Australia, but there could be many more dinosaur fossils waiting to be unearthed there. These countries were joined to all the other land masses of our planet at the time when dinosaurs first evolved, and so it is thought that many types of dinosaurs probably once existed there, too.

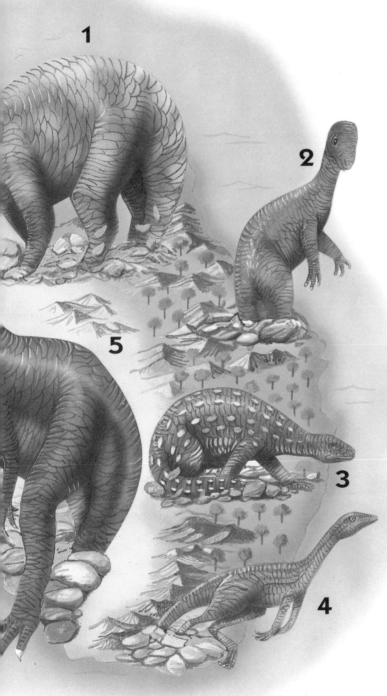

KEY

1 Muttaburrasaurus

2 Agrosaurus

3 Minmi

4 Leaellynosaurus

5 Allosaurus

6 Kakuru

Dinosaur

Remarkably, everything we now know about the dinosaurs has been discovered over the last 175 years or so. Prior to that, no one even knew that they had ever existed on our planet.

The very first discovery of dinosaur fossils was made in the 1820s in England; and not for another 30 years or so were any bones found in America, where more skeletal remains have since been unearthed than anywhere else in the world. Now they have been found in almost every corner of the globe.

BUILDING UP A PICTURE

As a result, scientists have gleaned an enormous amount of information about the world of the dinosaurs – gaining an impression of how they lived from day to day, how intelligent they were, how fast each species could run, what they looked like, and their bone structure. Scientists have also found out an enormous amount about the pterosaurs – flying reptiles that soared the prehistoric skies – and the plesiosaurs – enormous sea creatures that swam through the warm prehistoric seas.

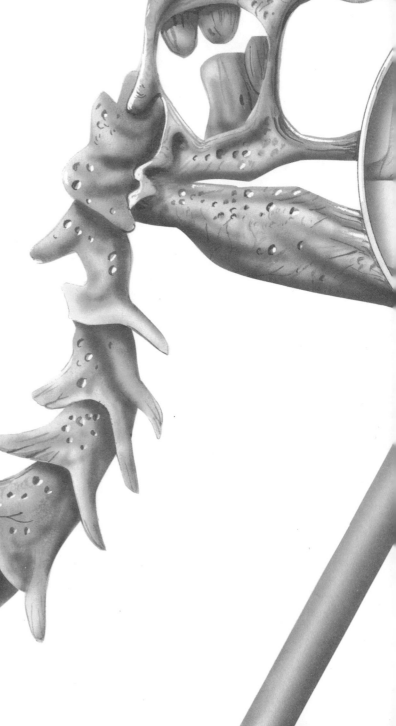

data

LIFE SPAN

We now know, too, quite a lot about how dinosaurs were born and the sort of life expectancy they had.

Growth rings in their fossilized bones suggest a span of at least eighty years for very large dinosaurs, and possibly a lot longer if, that is, they survived into adulthood. Most, however, would have perished before reaching maturity from illness or injury, or would have fallen prey to a carnivore of another species. Study of their skeletons also shows that some dinosaurs suffered from such diseases as arthritis or gout, and that they even developed tumors.

IN THEORY

Various theories about the relationship between dinosaurs and birds have been put forward. Paleontologists have come up with several suggestions, too, as to why the dinosaurs died out around 65 million years ago.

In the final section of this encyclopedia, you will find much more about these extraordinary beasts to marvel at, as we consider in detail many aspects of their 165-million-year existence on Planet Earth.

There are still several dinosaur puzzles remaining to be solved, however. Could it be that the next generation of paleontologists will succeed in clarifying these? If *your* interest in dinosaurs continues, might *you* perhaps one day come to number among them?

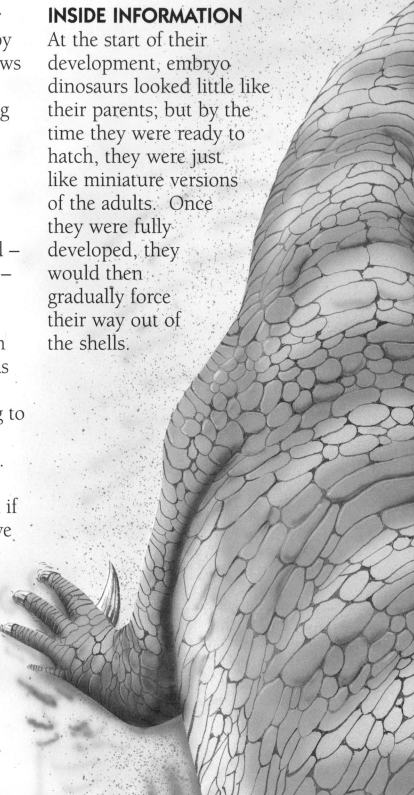

A mother Muttaburrasaurus sits guarding her nest and watches as her first baby hatches. Before too long, several other young will emerge as the eggs crack open, one by one.

Since the first discovery of dinosaur eggs in 1922 by an expedition led by paleontologist Roy Chapman Andrews to the Gobi Desert in Mongolia, scientists have succeeded in building up a fairly detailed picture of how baby dinosaurs developed.

LARGE CLUTCHES

Once a male and female had mated and the fertilized eggs had been laid – perhaps as many as twelve or more – an embryo dinosaur would start to grow in each. Nourishment was obtained from the yolk, and warmth from the mother incubating them, as well as from the sun.

If today's ostrich eggs are anything to go by, there was no danger that a mother dinosaur would crush them. (A man can sometimes stand on an ostrich egg without breaking it; and if you want to open one, you may have to drill it. Dinosaur eggs were probably even tougher.)

No one knows for sure, but it is likely that different species of dinosaurs had eggs of different sizes, colors and patterns, just as birds do. The nests, too, probably had many varied shapes.

INSIDE INFORMATION

At the start of their development, embryo dinosaurs looked little like their parents; but by the time they were ready to hatch, they were just like miniature versions of the adults. Once they were fully developed, they would then gradually force their way out of the shells.

dinosaur

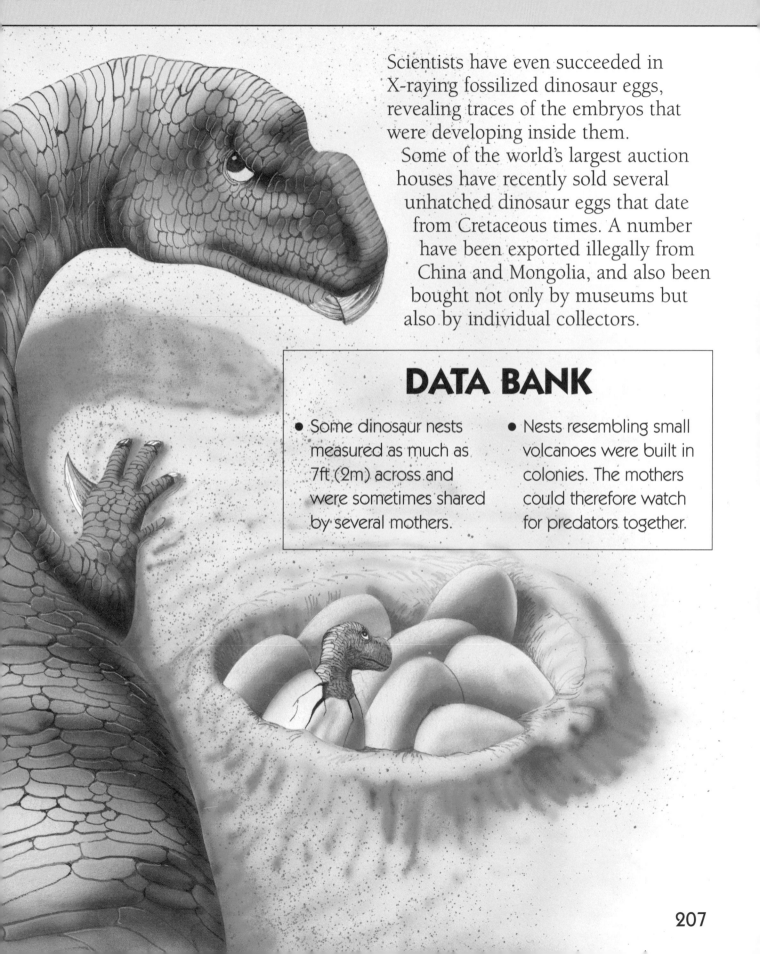

Scientists have even succeeded in X-raying fossilized dinosaur eggs, revealing traces of the embryos that were developing inside them.

Some of the world's largest auction houses have recently sold several unhatched dinosaur eggs that date from Cretaceous times. A number have been exported illegally from China and Mongolia, and also been bought not only by museums but also by individual collectors.

DATA BANK

- Some dinosaur nests measured as much as 7ft (2m) across and were sometimes shared by several mothers.

- Nests resembling small volcanoes were built in colonies. The mothers could therefore watch for predators together.

Dinosaur

A dinosaur as large as Brachiosaurus could easily have reached up to the fourth floor of an apartment building.

Some of the dinosaurs were undoubtedly the largest species ever to walk on Planet Earth. Today's giraffes, when fully grown, measure a mere 18ft (5.5m), while Brachiosaurus was about three times that height. It had an elongated neck that operated much like a crane does today. This enabled it both to browse on the very tallest of trees with ease and also to reach right down – to drink, perhaps, from a pool or river, or to check on its young.

BIG BONUS

Being big definitely had other advantages, too, for dinosaurs such as Brachiosaurus. Smaller species would be unlikely to attack, of course, unless trying to bring one down in a pack.

They could also probably have controlled their body temperature fairly well.

DOWN-SIDE

But there were disadvantages, too, in being huge. Movement was severely restricted. In fact, you only have to look at the pillar-like legs of Brachiosaurus to see that it could not have moved quickly. Obviously, the more weight a creature carries, the slower it is in moving around. (Brachiosaurus must have weighed about eight times as much as a T rex!)

DATA BANK

- A baby sauropod weighing very little when it hatched might have ended up weighing as much as 40 tons when fully mature – a startling increase in size.

size – 1

Such massive dinosaurs must also have had to have a very efficient circulatory system to pump sufficient blood all the way up to their brain.

How the earth must have shuddered when a herd of dinosaurs the size of Brachiosaurus were on the move! They would have ravaged the landscape, stripping trees bare as they sought huge amounts of food to satisfy their enormous appetites.

Dinosaur

A number of the dinosaurs were very small and actually quite ferocious little beasts, unlike Protoceratops, which might have made a good pet.

Because most of the best-known dinosaurs are either large and fierce or massive plant-eaters (T rex and Brachiosaurus, for example), it comes as something of a surprise to most people to learn for the first time that just as many dinosaurs were in fact very small in comparison.

PINT-SIZED

Take Protoceratops, for instance. As you can see from the illustration shown here, it was only about the height of a dog, and probably very tame and even-tempered.

But there were other even smaller dinosaurs – Compsognathus, for example – that were predatory carnivores, though only the size of a goose. If human beings had existed millions of years ago, in Late Jurassic times, this dinosaur, and others with a similar behaviour pattern – if pets – would have had to be muzzled for fear they might make use of their tremendously sharp teeth, and bite.

Other very small dinosaurs included Segisaurus (SEG-EE-SAW-RUS), a slim and swift predator dug up in Arizona, USA, and Procompsognathus, also a meat-eater, discovered in Germany.

Was life easier, then, for the larger or the smaller of the dinosaurs?

PROS AND CONS

Being little had its advantages, of course. A small dinosaur could move more speedily than its giant cousins; and the young probably did not need so much attention as they grew very quickly to adult size.

But there were risks, too. Predators were more likely to strike, and temperature control may have been a problem. Smaller dinosaurs also tended to be more finicky about food. If supplies were short, too, smaller creatures suffered more than the larger ones since they could not reach high into the treetops.

TINY HATCHLINGS

Only a very few dinosaur babies that emerged from a clutch of eggs probably survived to maturity. Perhaps this is not all that surprising, however, if you consider their size at birth. Newly hatched dinosaurs were tiny in comparison with their parents.

In some species, they could be as little as only several thousandth the size of the fully mature dinosaur, particularly in the case of a large sauropod, or even smaller. (A human newborn grows to only about four times its birth length, and that is only if it is finally fairly tall as an adult.)

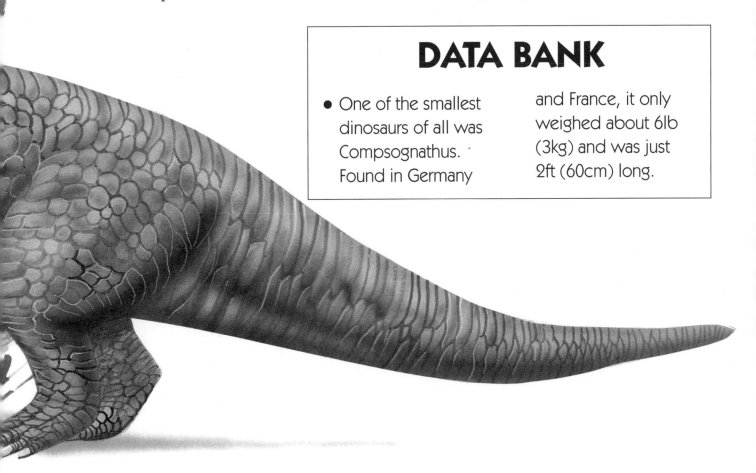

DATA BANK

- One of the smallest dinosaurs of all was Compsognathus. Found in Germany and France, it only weighed about 6lb (3kg) and was just 2ft (60cm) long.

Human beings have five senses: sight, smell, touch, hearing, and taste. And so did the dinosaurs, as scientists can tell from their remains.

From the eye sockets found in the skeletal remains of their skulls, we know that dinosaurs probably had fairly large eyes and so are likely to have had good sight. In general, their eyes were positioned towards the sides of their heads, as they were on Gallimimus, shown *below*. This would have helped it to spot any approaching predator, just as the keen-sighted predator would easily have been able to judge distance and stalk any likely prey.

LISTENING OUT

Dinosaurs did not have ears that look anything like yours but almost certainly could hear rather well through special slits. Scientists have even found the spot in some skulls that may have housed an eardrum. And, of course, they would roar to attract attention and so must have been heard. Parasaurolophus, *top right*, for instance, would bellow through its enormous head crest as a warning or threat, and possibly also to call to a female prior to mating.

LEATHERY

But dinosaurs probably lacked a good sense of touch as their skin was so thick and leathery. They might not even have felt very much if they were bitten by an insect. Their skin did, however, provide valuable protection in case of attack. And a victim would certainly have felt great pain when a sharply-clawed carnivore was out for the kill.

dinosaur senses

GREEDY BEASTS

Dinosaurs almost certainly had a good sense of taste, too. How a Tyrannosaurus rex, like the one *below*, must have salivated over the raw meat that it devoured in great lumps at each opportunity! And no doubt, too, herbivores chomped loudly and greedily on foliage, berries and other plant food.

DATA BANK

- Some scientists think that dinosaurs had color vision, although not all animals do.

- Some dinosaurs may also have had good nocturnal vision – useful if they hunted at night.

ON THE SCENT

Most carnivores would also have had a good sense of smell. Spinosaurus, shown *left*, for example, could easily sniff out a likely victim even at quite a distance, to judge by the large nasal openings that paleontologists have found in its fossilized skull.

How intelligent

We know from their fossilized remains that a great many dinosaurs were huge and would have towered way above you. But this does not mean they were necessarily big-brained.

No one has ever succeeded in digging up any dinosaur brains. But that is not surprising: brain tissue is too soft ever to become fossilized like bones. Even so, paleontologists have managed to obtain what they think is a fairly good impression of what they would have been like by studying the braincases of dinosaurs.

DINOSAUR DUNCE

The least intelligent dinosaur of all, according to current scientific opinion, may have been Stegosaurus, **1**. When it comes to calculating brainpower, it seems, the size of the brain itself, in comparison with body size, is what is all-important.

Simple Stegosaurus had a brain about the size of a walnut – tiny when you consider the bulk of its body.

LARGE BUT STUPID

The giant sauropods such as Apatosaurus, **2**, were bigger still than Stegosaurus but their brains were small, too, so they would not have done very well in any intelligence test either.

1

2

were dinosaurs?

THOUGHTLESS MONSTER

The ferocious carnivore Tyrannosaurus rex, **3**, had a brain that was actually larger than yours but the creature was still nowhere near as bright as you. Quite simply, the part used for thinking and reasoning, called the *cerebrum*, was only a small part of its brain. Other sections were larger, though, and helped it to hear and smell out victims very effectively.

SMALL BUT SMART

But the largest dinosaur brains of all belonged to much smaller, fast-footed, agile hunters such as Troodon, **4**. This comparatively tiny creature is likely to have been both crafty and intelligent, as dinosaurs go. Even then, its brain was only about one-thousandth of its body weight, whereas *your* brain is far, far larger in comparison with *your* body size.

DATA BANK

- The fossilized braincases of dinosaurs provide clues as to how intelligent they may have been.

- Experts think that some of the dinosaurs would have been no more intelligent than a snake, perhaps.

3

4

Which dinosaurs do experts think could run the fastest? And how have paleontologists been able to assess the speed of various types of dinosaurs?

If the distance between the fossilized footprints of dinosaurs is measured, together with their depth, scientists can get a reasonably accurate idea of the rate at which they moved. The fastest dinosaurs left great gaps between their strides as they sprinted along, for example. If such tracks are then compared with those of today's creatures whose top speeds are known, experts can estimate how fast each type of dinosaur could race, if it really generated speed.

REASONS FOR RUNNING

Dinosaurs usually needed to run at speed for one of two reasons – either to chase their prey or to escape from a predator. Hypsilophodon, **3**, for example, was a nifty little herbivore, perhaps able to reach up to 31mph (50km/h) to avoid an enemy. So fast was it for its size that the family to which it belongs has been nicknamed the "dinosaur gazelles."

SPRY SPRINTERS

Even faster were small ostrich-like creatures such as Gallimimus, **2**, which could have sprinted along comfortably at 37mph (60km/h). But perhaps the fastest dinosaur of all may have been Dromiceiomimus (DROM-EE-KEYE-OH-MIME-US), **1**, whose name means "emu mimic." You can see it winning the fantasy dinosaur race in the illustration shown here. This speed would surely have won it a gold medal if there had been dinosaur Olympics!

Many of the bigger dinosaurs could also break into a sprint, however, if necessary. Big, bulky Triceratops, **4**, for example, could probably have reached a rate of 30mph (48km/h) when charging.

speed

Tyrannosaurus rex, **5**, however, would have been somewhat slower.

LUMBERING GIANTS

The slowest dinosaurs of all would have been giant, long-necked sauropods like Diplodocus, **6**, seen here bringing up the rear. These extremely heavy creatures lumbered along at no more than 3.7mph (6km/h) – about the same as today's average human's walking pace. But even they could stampede in the attempt to escape from danger. Perhaps, as has been suggested recently with regard to the behavior of elephants, large plant-eating dinosaurs could even signal to each other by stamping a warning on the ground that could be heard from afar. Other dinosaurs of the species would then be alerted to any danger.

DATA BANK

- In general, dinosaurs with long, slim legs were, of course, the speediest of all.

- Dinosaurs with stiffened tails held them aloft when running.

5

3

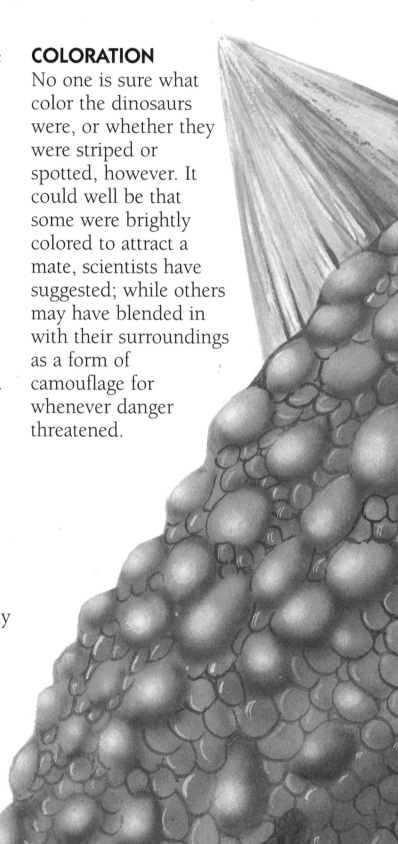

Dinosaur

Dinosaurs had no fur. Instead, their skin was the toughest of hide and probably extremely rough in texture, too. This would have helped protect them against predators.

When paleontologists first dug up the remains of Carnotaurus, there was huge excitement. Not only had they discovered an entirely new type of dinosaur, there were also impressions of its skin. Before then, only the trace of a small patch of theropod skin had ever been found.

GOOD IMPRESSIONS

The experts were so excited that they soon organized another expedition, hoping to discover more dinosaur skin. Looking in the same area, they found several more fossil impressions. In fact, they very soon had an excellent picture of what the skin would have looked like all over Carnotaurus' body and face.

BUMPS AND LUMPS

The fossil impressions show that the dinosaur's skin was very bumpy and that it was probably as tough as a rhino's hide. All over its body, the scaly skin had irregular, raised nodules, as you can see in this illustration of part of Carnotaurus' head. This would have stood up well to enemy attack, although few creatures probably dared to confront a ferocious Carnotaurus.

COLORATION

No one is sure what color the dinosaurs were, or whether they were striped or spotted, however. It could well be that some were brightly colored to attract a mate, scientists have suggested; while others may have blended in with their surroundings as a form of camouflage for whenever danger threatened.

Those dinosaurs that were carnivores had very differently shaped teeth from those that were plant-eaters, as you are about to find out.

Dilophosaurus, *below*, was a meat eater, and so had teeth sharp enough to tear at raw flesh. But the teeth of carnivores were not all the same size. Usually, the biggest carnivores had the largest teeth, and the most massive found so far belonged to Tyrannosaurus rex. Teeth that grew at the side of its mouth, near the front, were about the length of your lower leg, as you can see *below right*, and used for biting into prey.

CUTTING EDGE

In large carnivores, the curved edge of each tooth usually pointed backward. This gave them a better grip on their victims. Each tooth also usually had a serrated edge, like a saw, for cutting through meat; and, as the teeth wore away or perhaps broke off when biting too greedily into tough flesh, they would be replaced by new ones growing up from below.

teeth

SHARP BITE

By contrast, some small dinosaurs had teeth *smaller* than yours! Troodon, for instance – there are two of them in the third frame, *below* – had tiny, but incredibly sharp teeth, so that their bite would have been very painful indeed. In fact, the name *Troodon* means "wounding tooth."

Plant-eating dinosaurs had teeth more suited to coping with tough vegetation. Giants such as Diplodocus, *below*, did not chew their food.

Instead, they used peglike teeth for raking leaves into their mouths, and then swallowing them right away.

HUNDREDS OF TEETH

Some duck-billed dinosaurs, such as Edmontosaurus (ED-<u>MONT</u>-OH-<u>SAW</u>-RUS), *below*, had an enormous number of teeth – a great many more than adult humans of today. Just imagine how long it would take to brush your teeth twice a day if you had that many!

DATA BANK

- Some herbivores swallowed stones to help grind up the plant food that they ate.
- Dinosaur teeth were often self-sharpening and would regrow if damaged or lost.

Dinosaur

A beak was an important tool for dinosaurs that were herbivores and so had to snap off tough vegetation for their meals. It may also have served to give an enemy a nasty nip.

Scientists believe that Psittacosaurus, **1**, was an early relative of the *ceratopsids* – the family of dinosaurs with characteristic horns, frills and beaks. It had no horns and no real neck frill like Triceratops, **2**, – a Late Cretaceous true ceratopsid – had, however. But it certainly had a prominent beak like Triceratops'. In fact, the shape of its snout was so bird-like as you can see *below*, that the paleontologists who first discovered Psittacosaurus gave it a name with the meaning "parrot lizard."

PLANT-SLICER

Like Triceratops, Psittacosaurus would have had no trouble at all in slicing through thick-leaved plants.

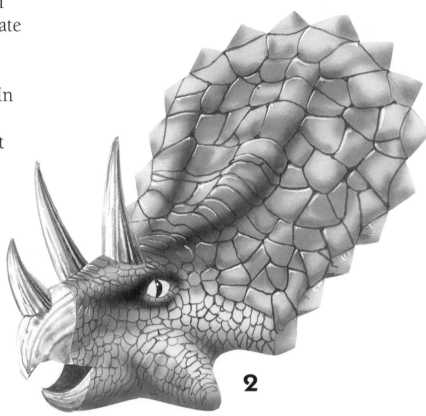

2

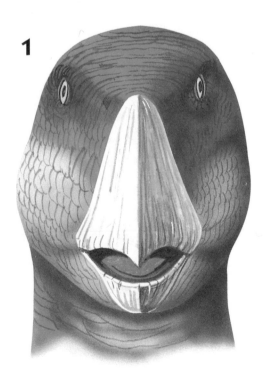

1

DATA BANK

- Beaked dinosaurs had a sharp bite and this seems to have survived in some of today's reptiles.

- Beaked dinosaurs usually had teeth, not at the front, but farther back inside their mouths.

beaks

Amazingly, even beaks as long as that of Ornithomimus (OR-NITH-OH-<u>MIME</u>-US), **3**, whose name means "bird mimic," were continually growing. Like other beaked dinosaurs, this speedy runner, which resembled an ostrich, always used its beak in the process of gathering food. So if it had not kept on growing – just as your nails do – the beak would have become worn down and useless in no time. Instead, continual regeneration meant it was always in good shape.

3

DUCK-BILLED

Dinosaur beaks were made from bone and had a horny coating to them. Edmontosaurus, **4** – called by this name because its remains were first dug up in Edmonton, a town in Canada – also had a horny coated beak, but this was rather more like a duck's bill in shape.

4

Unlike a duck, however, as you can also see on the previous two pages, Edmontosaurus, shown at the foot of this page, had hundreds of teeth farther back in its mouth, used for grinding up its intake of plant food.

Beaked dinosaurs may also have been able to store leaves in their cheeks, ready for later chewing.

PICKY EATERS

Some scientists have also suggested that the smaller beaked dinosaurs were possibly quite picky eaters, choosing only the most luscious-looking leaves and swallowing them quite delicately. What a contrast with the way that carnivores would have drooled over meat!

Various species of dinosaurs had finger and foot claws that were especially suited to their particular everyday needs.

Often it is the type of claw that a dinosaur has that provides a clue as to its identity. And sometimes a claw may be the very first fossil of a particular dinosaur to be dug up, the remaining bones not being unearthed until later. Such was the case with Baryonyx, on the *left* of the parade of dinosaurs, presented *below*. And no wonder it is often called Superclaw! Its thumb claw, **1**, one on each hand, was about the length of *your* whole arm. It was exceedingly sharp and experts believe it would have made a good fishing tool, as well as a defense weapon in case of attack.

Huge, long-necked, plant-eating Diplodocus, second in the line-up, also had a special claw, **2**. This was toward the inside of its front feet only and was also ideal for stabbing any predator that threatened it.

Deinonychus, however – third from the *left* – had a claw, **3**, that was a particularly brilliant piece of engineering.

1

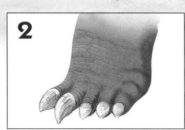

2

claws

SWITCHBLADE

When Deinonychus needed to slash at an enemy, balancing on one foot, it would proceed to swing the other leg so that its claw weapon could be put into action, much like a switchblade. The claw could then be retracted.

Noasaurus (NOE-A-<u>SAW</u>-RUS), fourth in the row, was only about 8ft (2.4m) long but still a fierce carnivore. Each foot had one larger, sharp claw, **4**, which was powered by strong muscles and used for attack.

Oviraptor was small for a dinosaur, too, but its strong three-fingered hands had large claws, **5**, which were handy for grasping things. True to its name, meaning "egg-thief," Oviraptor may have used the claws to pick up eggs stolen from other dinosaurs.

OUT FOR THE KILL

The slashing claws of predatory dinosaurs, males and females alike, were probably used to tear open the soft and vulnerable belly parts of their victims prior to the kill.

DATA BANK

- Some male dinosaurs may have stabbed at each other with sharp claws during duels.

- Two of Deinonychus' toes were weight-bearing: the third bore its killer claw.

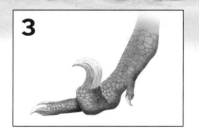

3

4

5

Many dinosaurs used sharp claws for protection. But some had rather unique forms of built-in weapons, on their heads or tails, for use when under attack from enemies.

Peaceful plant-eating dinosaurs had plenty of enemies among the terrifying carnivores. They therefore had to develop means of defending themselves. Some simply used speed to run away from danger. Others, however, were endowed with special features that enabled them to fight back with a vengeance.

Stegosaurus, **1**, for example – seen *below* in an encounter with an Allosaurus – sported magnificent weapons on its tail, something that must have come as a surprise to any assailant. If attacked, Stegosaurus would lash its tail around, as shown in the illustration, and the four pointed spikes that it bore would rip into the flesh of the predator.

Ankylosaurus, as you can see in the central illustration, had a most magnificent tail-club, one of the strongest dinosaur weapons of all. One swipe of this and an enemy would have been swept right off its feet or knocked unconscious.

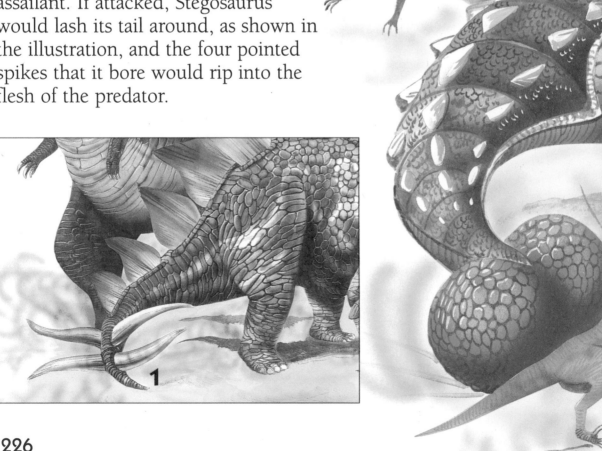

1

weapons

HEAD-TO-HEAD

Pachycephalosaurus had a skull that looked just like a bumpy dome and was exceedingly tough. This was just as well, because these normally gentle herbivores would engage in violent head-bashing sessions with others of their species from time to time, and may also have used their skulls most violently to charge at a predator.

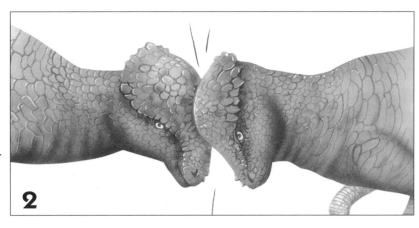

Triceratops, **3**, would use its three horns to fight an enemy, the two main ones measuring all of 3ft (90cm) in length. They would charge at a predator, digging these weapons deep into its flesh. They also fought among themselves, as shown, sparring just for fun or, more seriously, to determine who was the stronger and should therefore lead the herd or have mating rights with the females.

If their skulls had not been so thick, no doubt the Pachycephalosaurus, **2**, would have done themselves terrible harm when they fought in this way.

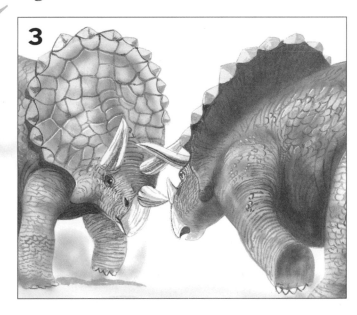

Dinosaur

All mammals are warm-blooded and that includes *you*. Reptiles, however, are cold-blooded. So what about the dinosaurs?

Some scientists think dinosaurs must have been cold-blooded. If this was the case, they would have had to participate actively in raising or lowering their body temperature. They may have done this by moving in and out of the sun, just as today's cold-blooded reptiles, such as crocodiles, do. Some dinosaurs such as Stegosaurus, **1**, may have used the plates on their backs to help them get warm or cool down, perhaps moving them up and down to help with this.

TEMPERATURE CONTROL

The sail on the back of an Ouranosaurus, **2**, may have served a similar purpose. On a chilly morning, Ouranosaurus may have stood broadside to the sun to allow its rays to warm the blood in its sail. Then, later in the day when it became too hot, Ouranosaurus may have stood edge-on to the sun to cool down.

It is also possible that some dinosaurs maintained their temperature level in another way. The large plant-eating sauropods, for instance, may have been able to store sufficient warmth in their massive bodies to see them through the night, when the temperature probably went down considerably. The huge amounts of food they took in almost certainly generated a lot of heat in the process of digestion. And since they were so big and heavy, simply walking around must have required a lot of energy, in turn increasing their body temperature.

1

A MATTER OF SPEED

We also know that many dinosaurs – Gallimimus, **3**, for instance – could run for great distances and at very high speed, and so were probably warm-blooded.

Today's reptiles can only move in shorter bursts because they are cold-blooded and, as a result, do not have enough energy for great activity.

2

DATA BANK

- Some scientists think that dinosaurs were warm-blooded or 'endothermic' because they were just as active as mammals.

- A number of dinosaurs possibly had built-in "solar panels" in the form of plates and sails to help regulate temperature.

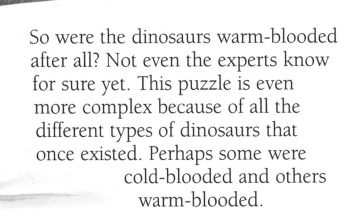

3

So were the dinosaurs warm-blooded after all? Not even the experts know for sure yet. This puzzle is even more complex because of all the different types of dinosaurs that once existed. Perhaps some were cold-blooded and others warm-blooded.

Dinosaur

Ever since dinosaurs were first discovered, scientists have tried to come up with an accurate picture of what these amazing creatures were like. It has not always been straightforward, however.

With only incomplete skeletons to work from in most cases, a few odd theories have arisen among paleontologists from time to time as to the appearance and behavior of the many different species of dinosaur. One of the strangest concerned the plant-eater Hypsilophodon.

Over one hundred years ago, the British scientist James Hulke declared that, because the remains of Hypsilophodon showed it had long fingers and toes, it must have been well-suited to climbing. He therefore announced that Hypsilophodon, and possibly other dinosaurs with similar body forms, lived in trees.

UP A GUM TREE?

Other scientists came to agree with him after deciding that, since Hypsilophodon's first toes pointed in a different direction from its others, they must have been particularly useful for gripping, and therefore the creature could have used them for climbing into trees, and swinging from one to the other. Hypsilophodon, it was also said, had arched claws rather like today's tree kangaroos, which would have made walking on the ground quite awkward.

In the 1970s, however, British paleontologist Peter Galton began to put together the bones of Hypsilophodon in a new way, and showed that all its toes in fact faced in the same direction. Its feet were not those of a tree dweller after all.

NIMBLE-FOOTED

Experts now agree that Hypsilophodon's long limbs were in fact those of a fast runner. Its stiff tail helped it keep its balance when moving at speed. Animals that live in trees need flexible tails for gripping: a stiff tail would almost certainly get in the way when climbing.

So, today, no paleontologist believes that Hypsilophodon – nor any other dinosaur for that matter – lived in trees but on the ground, as shown in this illustration, in which several of the species are trying to escape from the waters of a sudden flood after heavy rain.

Judging from their fossilized skulls, some dinosaur heads seem to have been so spectacular that they were infinitely more outrageous than any of today's high-fashion hats.

Which of the dinosaurs featured on the following four pages do you think had the most remarkable head?

Parasaurolophus, **1**, shown *below*, sported an extremely long crest through which it could bellow like a fog horn.

Other dinosaurs had distinctive features on their heads, such as. Stegoceras (STEG-<u>OSS</u>-ERR-ASS), **2**.

It had a bony, dome-shaped skull which experts believe it may have used very forcefully in head-banging fights with other Stegoceras. These usually took place in set-piece battles during which they fought over territory, over leadership of the herd or over female Stegoceras during the mating season, much as modern stags engage in rutting behavior today.

1

This crest, sometimes described as a hollow tube, extended to all of 4ft (1.3m) in length, so that it was approximately *your* height, or even taller. The noise it is thought that Parasaurolophus was able to make through this bony protrusion sounded long, low and loud, experts believe. It would have been audible over some considerable distance, and may have provided a ready warning to other Parasaurolophus, in the event of approaching danger.

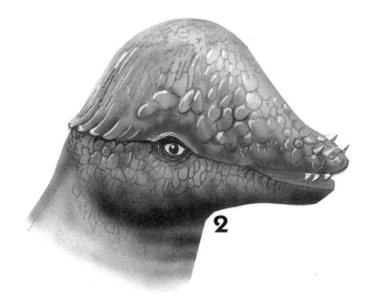

2

wonderful heads

Styracosaurus, **3**, was a heavily-built dinosaur with a head surrounded by a huge frill from which six large spines rose proudly – hence its name, meaning "spiked-lizard." Styracosaurus certainly must have had a very frightening appearance and few dinosaurs probably therefore dared attack it. The sharp and lengthy head spikes may also have been used to ward off rivals for females of the same species; and its prominent nose horn, too, would have made a good defense weapon.

3

NATURAL HELMET

Shamosaurus (SHAM-OH-<u>SAW</u>-RUS), **4**, was an armored dinosaur with tough spikes just behind and to the sides of its eyes for protection. The skin on its head was exceedingly bumpy, too, paleontologists believe, providing it with a sort of protective helmet as part of its natural body covering. More weird and wonderful dinosaur heads are featured on the next page.

DATA BANK

- Males and females of the same species may sometimes have had heads of a different size or different skin coloring, the males probably being more spectacular.

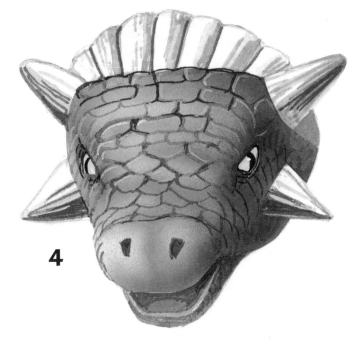

4

Most sauropods – the giant long-necks – had very small and rather insignificant skulls for their body-build. Other dinosaurs, however, had highly decorative heads.

Pachycephalosaurus, **1**, a bone-headed dinosaur, had all sorts of bumpy bits of bone surrounding the close-fitting skull cap that crowned its head.

This tall plant-eater was generally peaceful and spent nearly all its time feeding. But, like all the bone-heads, it would-engage in head-to-head contests which may have developed into quite violent encounters as their skulls crashed noisily. But at least their eyes were protected by a rim of bony protrusions around the base of the cap.

THREE HORNS

Triceratops, **2**, is known for the three horns from which it gets its name. Two were over its eyes, and there was a single smaller one above its beak.

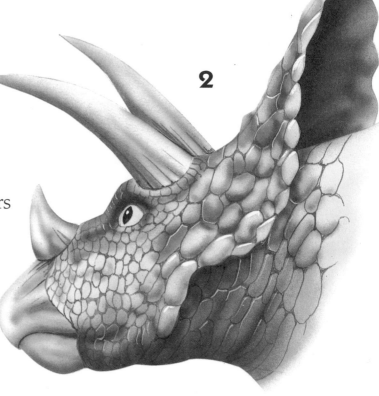

Triceratops' snout was shaped rather like a parrot's beak, and would have been put to good use for slicing up its copious meals of vegetable stuff.

Behind its two larger horns, meanwhile, Triceratops had a large, bony frill with a wavy edge that framed its face, rather like the huge ruffs that were worn as neckwear in Elizabethan times.

wonderful heads

LONG JAW

Chirostenotes (KY-ROW-STEN-<u>OH</u>-TEEZ), **3**, a small, two-legged dinosaur, had a plainer but very individually-designed head, as you can see, *below*.

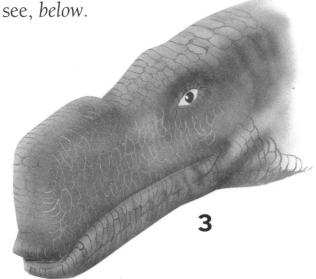

3

Just look at that long, deep jaw with its extraordinary bulging upper part!

SINGLE SPIKE

From the top of the head of Tsintaosaurus (ZIN-TAY-OH-<u>SAW</u>-RUS), **4** – a large herbivore – rose an unusual, single spike that pointed slightly forward, so that the effect was something like a feather sticking up from a head-hugging hat. Stranger and stranger...

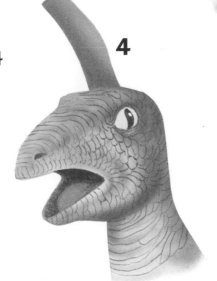

4

As you can see, the large hadrosaur Lambeosaurus (LAM-BE-OH-<u>SAW</u>-RUS), **5**, had a skull with a most peculiar hatchet-shaped crest rising from it. This crest, some scientists think, was larger and more colorful in the males and so may have played a part in sexual display, just as today's peacocks will put on a show for peahens prior to mating.

5

DATA BANK

- The depth of Triceratops' head alone was greater than *your* height.

- Some dinosaur crests were hollow and used for making calling sounds.

Dinosaur

Dinosaurs have been extinct for many millions of years, but we can still learn a lot about them, not only from their skeletons but also from the tracks they left when walking in wet mud.

footprints

As well as finding fossilized dinosaur bones, eggs and nests, paleontologists have also discovered a number of dinosaur footprints in various locations all over the world.

From these, experts can tell whether the creatures that left them walked on two legs or four, how many toes they had, if they had claws and, judging by their stride, how big they were.

ON THE TRACK

Scientists can even assess the speed of various types of dinosaurs, by measuring both the distance between the prints and their depth, as well as whether they lived in herds, from the number of prints.

The very best prints found so far come from long-necked herbivores, such as Diplodocus, seen here in the distance. Footprints of ferocious carnivores, such as Ceratosaurus, shown stalking the herd of Diplodocus in this illustration, have also been found in the eastern foothills of the Rocky Mountains of North America.

DATA BANK

- Some dinosaur footprints are nearly as wide as *you* are tall!

- The deeper the footprint, the heavier the dinosaur is likely to have been.

237

Scavengers

Most carnivorous dinosaurs would kill for meat. But sometimes, if they were lucky, they would find corpses to feed on.

When a herd of plant-eaters, such as Chasmosaurus, found fresh vegetation in a lush valley, they would feed contentedly for hours on end. Yet, at any time, the peace of a Cretaceous afternoon could be broken. Sudden rain storms sometimes developed into flash floods without any warning whatsoever.

A great wall of muddy water might then rush down to the valley, drowning everything in its path. A herd of dinosaurs feeding in such an area had no chance of escape.

They would all be swept away and perish in the deluge. Once the waters had subsided, scavenging dinosaurs would be after an easy meal. Such meat-eaters had great jaws and sharp teeth, perfect for pulling away tough flesh from the carcass of a dead dinosaur.

Several may even have fought over pieces of flesh. After a day or two, all that would be left would be gnawed and scattered bones.

In the prehistoric

Dinosaurs ruled the Earth for about 160 million years. Other creatures, meanwhile, ruled the skies. They were not birds but pterosaurs.

In his book *The Lost World*, Sir Arthur Conan Doyle imagines spotting some pterosaurs which, amazingly, had survived from prehistoric times. "*It was a wonderful sight to see at least a hundred creatures of enormous size and hideous appearance all swooping like swallows ... above us,*" he wrote.

The very first pterosaurs lived about 230 million years ago in the Triassic era, long before the first birds. Although they were very different, some scientists think that pterosaurs and dinosaurs both evolved from the same early creatures.

Some pterosaurs were large; others were tiny, as small as a robin. Some had strong muscles and could flap their wings to fly. Others, however, probably had to rely on currents of air to help them glide along.

WINGED REPTILES

There were two main types of pterosaur or winged reptiles. One of these, the Rhamphorhynchoids (RAM-FO-RIN-KOIDS) – their name means "prow beaks" – had long jaws, sharp teeth, short necks and lengthy tails. Some also had fur covering their bodies to keep them warm.

The other group, the Pterodactyloids (TER-OH-DACT-EEL-OIDS) – their name means "winged fingers" – had shorter tails but longer beaks and, again, sharp teeth. Pterodactylus (TER-OH-DACT-EEL-US), shown here, belonged to this family and had an extremely long fourth finger supporting each wing.

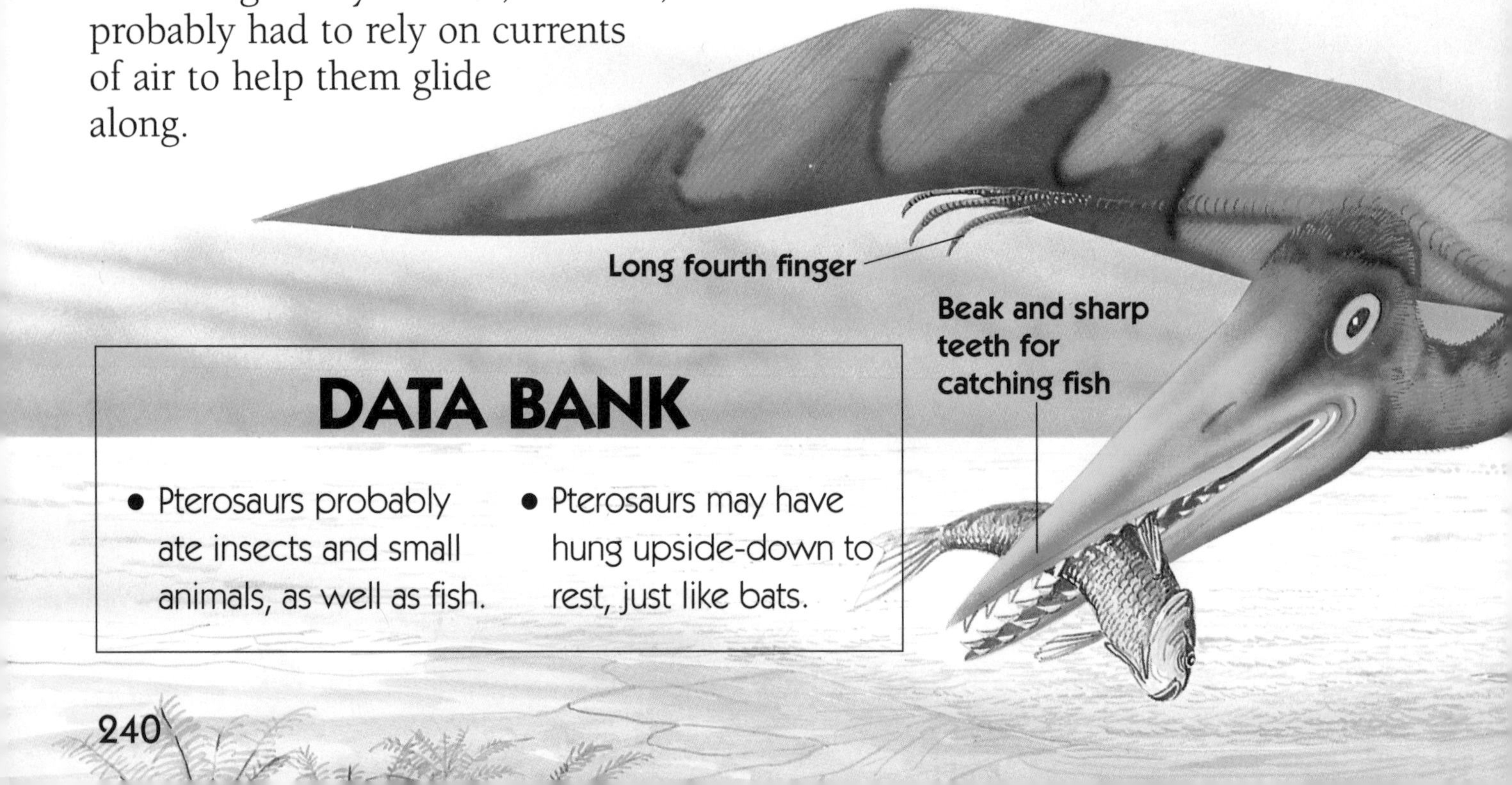

Long fourth finger

Beak and sharp teeth for catching fish

DATA BANK

- Pterosaurs probably ate insects and small animals, as well as fish.

- Pterosaurs may have hung upside-down to rest, just like bats.

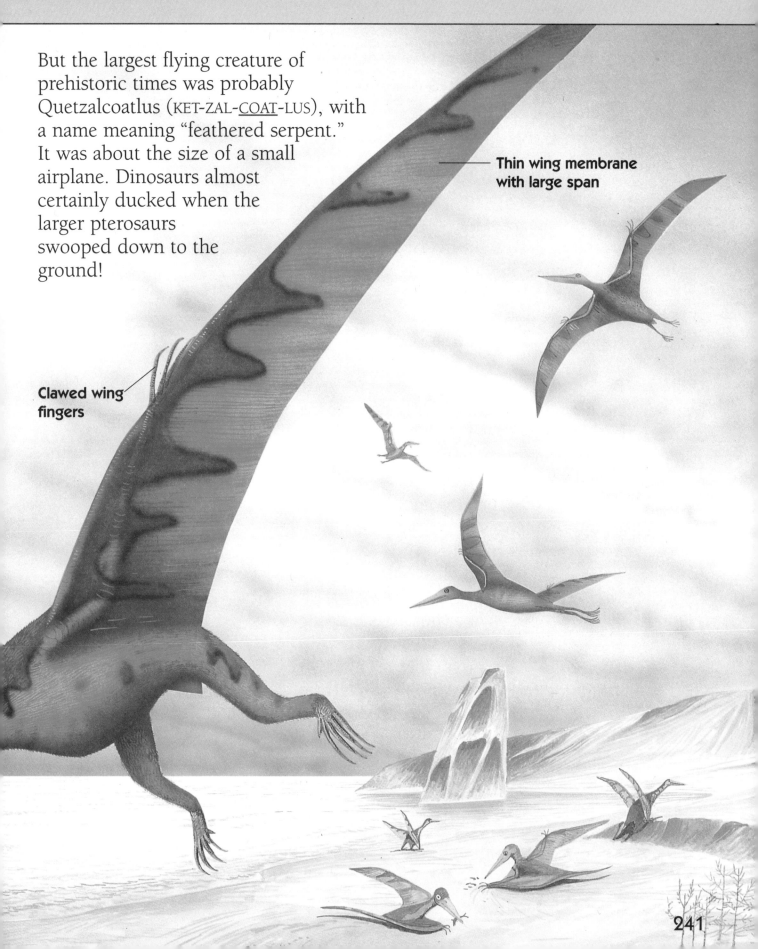

But the largest flying creature of prehistoric times was probably Quetzalcoatlus (KET-ZAL-<u>COAT</u>-LUS), with a name meaning "feathered serpent." It was about the size of a small airplane. Dinosaurs almost certainly ducked when the larger pterosaurs swooped down to the ground!

Thin wing membrane with large span

Clawed wing fingers

So far, paleontologists have discovered the remains of pterosaurs in places as far apart as Europe, Africa, and North and South America. Indeed, they probably once existed worldwide.

There seem to have been many different types of pterosaur in prehistoric times; but most had certain things in common, even if they varied considerably in size. Those that were built for flight had light, hollow bones to keep their weight down, and wings as thin as rubber bands, for instance.

KEEN-EYED

They also probably had good eyesight, enabling them to see for long distances. It was important to spot potential danger well in advance, and also any prey that would make a good meal. Most pterosaurs, however, were not designed to walk with ease on the ground, and could only balance gingerly whenever they landed.

Pterodactylus, **3**, lived about 150 million years ago in Late Jurassic times. Some scientists think that, like certain other pterosaurs, it may have had a throat pouch, much like a pelican's. This would have been used to store any small fish that it brought to its young. Its tail was short, but it had a wing span that was larger than a double bed; and like others of its family group, it was covered with soft hair but had smooth wings.

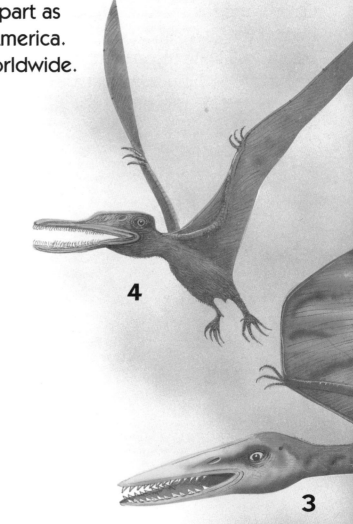

TOOTHY PTEROSAURS

Sharp teeth were a feature of many pterosaurs. Ctenochasma (TEN-OH-KAZ-MAH), **1**, for instance, though half the size of Pterodactylus, had as many as 260 inward-curving teeth. No wonder scientists gave it a name meaning 'comb jaw'! Such fine teeth would have proved very useful indeed for filtering out any unwanted bits, such as bones, when feeding.

prehistoric skies

BONY HEAD CRESTS

Gallodactylus (GAL-OH-DAK-TEE-LUS), **2**, known for its head crest, has a name meaning "Gallic finger" since it was first found in France – *Gallic* means "French." Unlike most other pterosaurs, it only had teeth at the front of its long jaws.

Germanodactylus (JER-MAN-OH-DAK-TEE-LUS), **4**, was given a name meaning "German finger" because it was first found in Germany. It, too, had a thin, bony crest on top of its head; and, like the other two small pterosaurs in this illustration, would have been dwarfed by its close cousin, Pterodactylus. All of them were strong fliers and yet were not birds, as you will discover elsewhere in this encyclopedia.

DATA BANK

- Some pterosaurs may perhaps have had webbed feet for paddling in water.

- Pterosaurs almost certainly regurgitated food in order to feed their young.

Prehistoric

All sorts of reptiles swam in the warm prehistoric oceans, searching constantly for food by chasing shoals of fish or crunching on shells.

While dinosaurs dominated the land, marine reptiles, such as Plesiosaurus (PLEA-SEA-OH-SAW-RUS), shown here, spent their whole lives in the waters of shallow seas or lagoons. About the length of a small car, they had an amazingly long neck and tail, and a round, barrel-shaped body.

One scientist has even described them as being like snakes threaded through turtles. In 1814, an almost complete fossilized skeleton was found in soft, crumbling cliffs in England.

Four strong flippers for swimming

Thick, lengthy tail

ocean life

From these remains, discovered by Mary Anning, we know that it had rows of sharp teeth, and that strong muscles attached four thick flippers to its body. Experts estimate its weight at about fourteen times that of today's average human being.

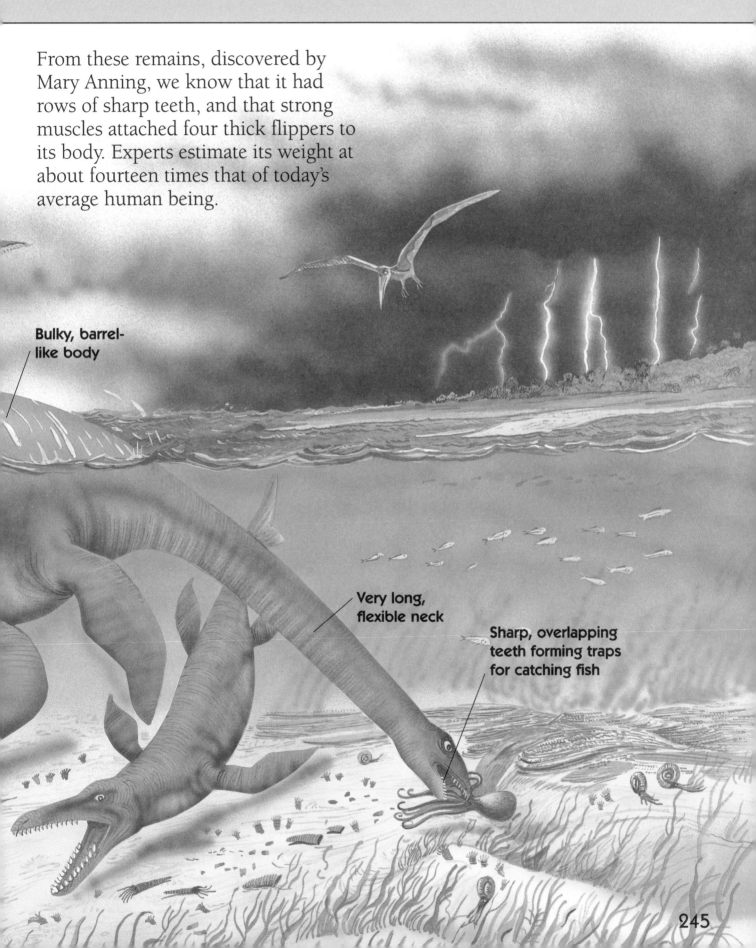

Bulky, barrel-like body

Very long, flexible neck

Sharp, overlapping teeth forming traps for catching fish

For hundreds of years, there have been rumors about enormous creatures that lurk in lakes worldwide – Ogopogo, Slimy Sid and the Loch Ness Monster, for example. Some people even believe they may be survivors from prehistoric times, though most scientists think this unlikely.

Scientists have found the fossilized remains of several different underwater creatures that date from the age of the dinosaurs. From examination of its bones, it is known that a fully-grown Plesiosaurus, **4**, for instance, was about the size of a small car.

It weighed many times as much as *you* do. It was by no means the largest of the plesiosaur family, however, as you can see from this illustration. Some were absolute giants of the deep and more than ten times the size of Plesiosaurus.

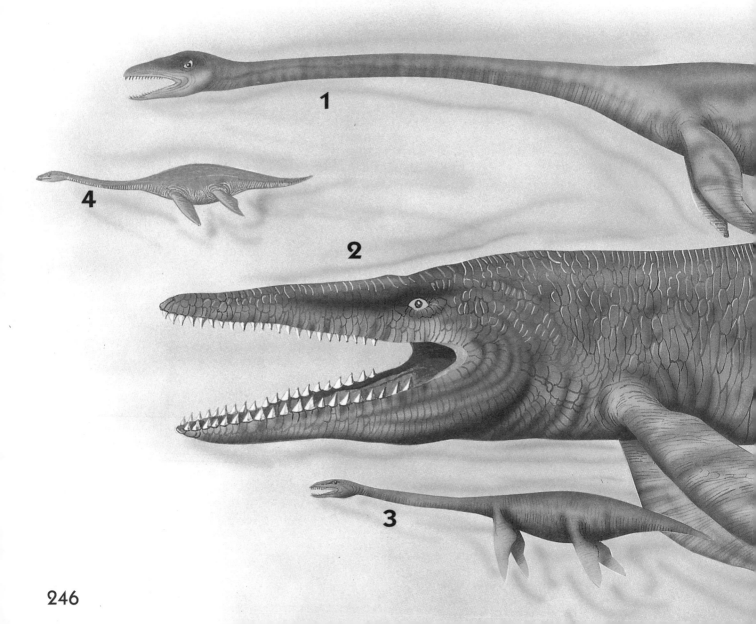

prehistoric seas

FISH TRAP

Cryptoclidus (KRIP-TOE-KLY-DUS), **3**, lived about 170 million years ago in Jurassic times. Its remains show that, when its jaws closed, the teeth overlapped, making a very useful built-in fish trap.

Elasmosaurus (EE-LASS-MOE-SAW-RUS), **1**, lived about 70 million years ago. Its head was small but it had many sharp teeth – all the better to gobble up unsuspecting marine creatures.

Kronosaurus (KRONE-OH-SAW-RUS), **2**, may only have had a short neck, but it was tremendously thick. Its jaws, were massive, and it probably ate other plesiosaurs, as well as huge amounts of fish several times each day.

In fact, the chances are it hardly ever stopped eating! It was, you might say, the Jaws of the prehistoric seas.

DATA BANK

- Plesiosaurs probably laid their eggs in holes in the sand, just like turtles do today.

- They would dive into the water and come up three or four times each hour to breathe.

- Dinosaurs may sometimes have plunged into water to catch food or to escape predators but could not swim like the plesiosaurs.

Read on to discover which dinosaurs would deserve a place in any prehistoric book of records, and why. You could be in for a few surprises as we introduce some dinosaur "stars."

Megalosaurus surely merits a place in any listing of dinosaur records. After all, it was the first to be discovered when its thigh bone, **1**, was found in 1677, although not recognized.

LONGEST NECK

Mamenchisaurus, meanwhile, dug up in China, and a plant-eater, had what is thought to be the world's longest neck ever, extending all of 32ft (10m). In fact, its neck extended to more than half its total body length and measured more than eight times the height of today's average adult man.

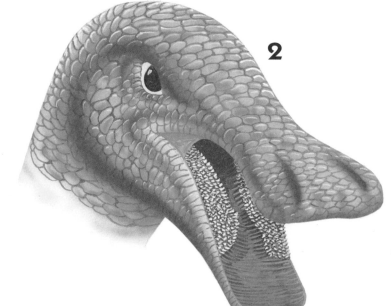

TOOTHY BEASTS

Once you have all *your* second teeth, there will be 32 of them. Behind their toothless beaks, duck-billed dinosaurs, **2**, however, had lots more – as many as 480 in the upper and another 480 in the lower jaw!

DATA BANK

- The longest dinosaur name of all is Micropachycephalosaurus (MY-CROW-PAK-EE-CEFF-A-LOW SAW-RUS), which means "tiny thick-headed lizard."

- Because new teeth came through when old ones broke or wore down, some dinosaurs may have grown as many as 10,000 in a lifetime.

records

MIGHTIEST OF ALL

Built like a tank, Ankylosaurus, **3**, which roamed North America in Late Cretaceous times, had an amazing armored head and body.

3

Reinforcement was provided by several rows of nasty-looking plates and spikes. Its tail was powerful, too, ending in a strange, two-sectioned bony club. This was ideal for swiping at enemies that came too close. Even dinosaurs as ferocious as Tyrannosaurus rex had to beware of this mighty monster or risk a fatal blow from its tail. Ankylosaurus was an herbivore, however, and did not kill for food, only striking when threatened.

HEAVYWEIGHT

From the size of its skeletal remains, scientists have calculated that, when fleshed-out, Ultrasaurus (<u>ULL</u>-TRA-<u>SAW</u>-RUS), **4** – a Late Jurassic dinosaur from Colorado in North America – may have weighed as much as 55 tons – that's many times as much as today's elephants. It may also have been one of the tallest dinosaurs, standing at about six times higher than an average bedroom ceiling! It seems it was possible for some types of dinosaur to grow big and strong without eating meat.

4

Dinosaurs

Could it really be that the sparrow hopping about on your lawn and the eagle soaring through the skies are both descended from the dinosaurs?

Dinosaurs, as far as we know, had no feathers; and most certainly looked little like most of the birds of today's world. Yet many experts are convinced that dinosaurs and birds are related.

It all started back in 1926 when the Danish scientist Gerhard Heilmann published a book in which he presented the skeletons of both dinosaurs and birds, pointing out that there were in fact similarities, just as British scientist Thomas Huxley had thought. The body of a Struthiomimus (STROOTH-EE-OH-<u>MIME</u>-US), for instance, he said, was much like that of an ostrich. He did have a few doubts, however, as to whether both belonged to the same family because dinosaurs – as far as paleontologists knew at the time – had no collar bones but birds do.

More recently, Professor John Ostrom has also compared the skeleton of the earliest known bird, Archaeopteryx (AR-KEE-<u>OP</u>-TER-ICKS), shown here, and the small dinosaur, Compsognathus, from Late Jurassic times. He, too, found a number of similarities, and that some dinosaurs did have collar bones after all.

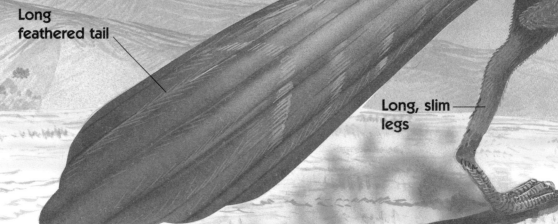

Long feathered tail

Long, slim legs

and birds

JUST A FLUTTER

Archaeopteryx was first discovered in Germany back in 1861. Remains show that it had small, pointed teeth, but no beak, a long tail, and probably could not fly very well.

Instead, it just fluttered around to catch dragonflies and other insects for food, as in this illustration, or climbed trees. Its wings were in fact more like feathered, fingered arms; but its legs and feet, and hips, were very similar to those of certain dinosaurs.

Recently, however, fossils of other primitive birds – dating from *before* the time when Archaeopteryx lived – have been discovered in China. This has therefore caused some scientists to question whether Archaeopteryx marks a definite link beween dinosaurs and birds.

Dragonfly

Feathered arms

Dinosaur-like feet

DATA BANK

- We know that Archaeopteryx had feathers because fossilized prints of them were found near to the site of its skeletal remains.
- A South American bird called the hoatzin has claws on its wings, just like Archaeopteryx, and also climbs trees.

About 65 million years ago, all the dinosaurs seem suddenly to have disappeared. Scientists continue to present new theories as to why this might have happened.

During the 1970s, Nobel Prize winner Luis Alvarez and his son began studying some rather odd rock formations in Italy. These contained a very high proportion of *iridium*, a metal that is rare on Earth but abundant in outer space. The rocks dated from around 65 million years ago, when dinosaurs are thought to have become extinct. Could there perhaps have been some connection?

TERRIFIC IMPACT

Alvarez wondered whether an asteroid – a giant chunk of rock from elsewhere in the Universe – might perhaps have hit the Earth. As a result, thick clouds of dust may have blotted out all sunlight for a considerable length of time, so that plants could not grow and all the dinosaurs starved to death as a result.

Other experts differ and maintain that dinosaurs disappeared when sea levels rose and caused dreadful floods, or that a star may have exploded, showering the Earth with deadly rays.

But whichever of these theories is the most accurate, it is puzzling that some creatures actually managed to survive.

DATA BANK

- No dinosaur remains have been found in rocks that are younger than 65 million years old.

- Dinosaurs became extinct due to some form of global catastrophe.

extinction

Glossary

Abelisaurids – a family of predatory dinosaurs

amber – fossilized tree sap

Ankylosaurids – a family of armored dinosaurs

ankylosaurs – quadrupedal, armored dinosaurs

archosaurs – advanced reptiles, including crocodiles and dinosaurs

asteroid – a giant chunk of rock from outer space

bipedal – walking on two legs

cannibal – any animal that eats its own kind

carnivore – a meat-eater

carnosaur – a large, bipedal theropod

casts – fossils comprising different materials from the original bones

Ceratopsids – members of a large family of dinosaurs, including Triceratops and Chasmosaurus

cerebrum – part of the brain used for thinking and reasoning

coelurosaurs – small, bipedal saurischian dinosaurs

coprolites – fossilized droppings or excrement

Cretaceous – the third and last age of the dinosaurs, lasting from 144-65 million years ago

cycads – tropical plants wih fern-like leaves

DNA – gives all life forms their hereditary characteristics

Dromaeosaurids – a family of dinosaurs, all speedy hunters

fossil – the remains of a plant or animal from a past age, preserved in rock

gastroliths – stones swallowed by herbivores to help digestion

ginkgoes – small trees with fan-shaped leaves

gizzard – a bulge in the gut where food is ground up

glycogen – a chemical released to supply extra energy

Gondwana - part of the 'supercontinent' of Pangaea

hadrosaurs – large ornithopods with duck-like beaks

herbivore – a plant-eater

hoatzin – a South American bird

horsetails – plants with small, tooth-like leaves

ichnites – fossilized tracks

iridium – a very hard metal, rare on Earth but abundant in outer space

Jurassic – the second age of the dinosaurs, lasting from 208-145 million years ago

Laurasia – part of the 'supercontinent' of Pangaea

Morrison Formation – a site in Colorado, USA, where many important dinosaur finds have been made

molds – holes in rock after bones have decomposed

ooliths – fossilized eggs

ornithischians – the 'bird-hipped' dinosaurs, all herbivores

ornithomimosaurs – a group of dinosaurs with slender limbs and toothless beaks, all fast runners

ornithopods – plant-eating ornithischians, mostly bipedal

paleontologist – an expert in the study of prehistoric remains

Pangaea – the great 'supercontinent' that existed before land on Earth started to divide up

Panthalassa – a single great ocean that existed in prehistoric times

Plateosaurids – an early family of dinosaurs, all herbivores

plesiosaur – a prehistoric sea creature

prosauropod – a very early form of sauropod, dating from Triassic times

pterodactyl – a type of winged reptile from prehistoric times

Pterodactyloids – types of winged reptiles

pterosaur – any of several types of winged reptile from prehistoric times

quadrupedal – walking on four limbs

Rhamphorhynchoids – types of winged reptiles

saurischians – the 'lizard-hipped' dinosaurs, some of which were herbivores, some carnivores

sauropods – large, long-necked, long-tailed quadrupedal dinosaurs, mostly from Jurassic times

tendon – tough tissue attaching muscle to bone

theropods – a group of bipedal, flesh-eating saurischian dinosaurs

trace fossils – fossils of tracks and droppings, rather than of an animal itself

Triassic – the first age of the dinosaurs, lasting from 220-209 million years ago

Index